HILARION
THE HEALER

Meet the Master Series

Afra—Brother of Light

Saint Germain—Master Alchemist

Hilarion the Healer—The Apostle Paul Reborn

MEET THE MASTER SERIES

HILARION
THE HEALER
The Apostle Paul Reborn

*Teachings of Mark L. Prophet
and Elizabeth Clare Prophet*

compiled by
The Editors of The Summit Lighthouse Library

THE SUMMIT LIGHTHOUSE LIBRARY®

HILARION THE HEALER: THE APOSTLE PAUL REBORN
Teachings of Mark L. Prophet and Elizabeth Clare Prophet
compiled by the editors of The Summit Lighthouse Library
Copyright © 2004 Summit Publications, Inc. All rights reserved

For information, contact Summit University Press,
63 Summit Way, Gardiner, MT 59030.
Tel: 1-800-245-5445 or 406-848-9500
Web site: www.SummitUniversityPress.com
E-mail: info@SummitUniversityPress.com

Library of Congress Control Number: 2004111061
ISBN: 978-0-922729-80-7 (softbound)
ISBN: 978-1-932890-49-5 (eBook)

THE SUMMIT LIGHTHOUSE LIBRARY®
The Summit Lighthouse Library is an imprint of Summit University Press.

SUMMIT UNIVERSITY 🐚 PRESS®

Summit University Press, 🐚, The Summit Lighthouse Library,
The Summit Lighthouse, *Pearls of Wisdom*, Keepers of the Flame, and
Science of the Spoken Word are trademarks registered in the U.S. Patent
and Trademark Office and in other countries. All rights reserved

Some images copyright © 2004 Jupiterimages Corporation

Cover image: Paul Preaching to the Thessalonians, by Gustave Doré

IMPORTANT NOTE: The ascended masters do not recommend the
avoidance of established medical procedures. Nor do they recommend the
application of any healing technique without the advice and supervision of
a licensed health care practitioner. The masters encourage the prevention
of illness through natural methods, including a disciplined diet, exercise,
fresh air, a positive spiritual and mental attitude and wise health care in
every area of living. However, this is not a substitute for medication and the
proper medical care under a physician when needed.

Printed in the United States of America

15   14   13   12   11   6   5   4   3   2

Meet the Master

When the pupil is ready, the teacher appears.

There is a brotherhood of light—masterful beings who have graduated from earth's schoolroom. These masters are wayshowers, guiding us on the path home to God. From the heaven-realm, they assist mankind in all fields of human endeavor, helping to raise the consciousness of earth.

Each master is also a teacher in search of a student, desiring to reach from beyond the veil to touch that one for the acceleration of their spiritual evolution. The *Meet the Master* series seeks to introduce the student to the master. ⚜

Meet the Master Hilarion

Saint Hilarion was the fourth-century healer and hermit who founded monasticism in Palestine. He had previously been embodied as the apostle Paul, who, as Saul of Tarsus, met Jesus on the road to Damascus and was both blinded and later healed by the light of the Master Physician.

Saint Hilarion had the gift of healing in abundant measure, learned from the heart of his Saviour, Jesus. Toward the end of his life, he lived in the desert of Cyprus, having moved to this remote part of the world in order to escape the crowds who sought relief through the fountain of healing that flowed from him. But it was not possible for the "people's saint," as he was called, to evade the people—the multitudes followed him wherever he went. Finally his Lord taught him that the gift of truth and healing is only for the sharing, for the giving away. And so he healed.

Today from the ascended realm, Hilarion continues his healing mission. As the master of healing and truth, he is accessible to all who desire healing, teaching the way of self-healing and the rules of healing not only of the body, but of the mind, soul and spirit. ⚜

Table of Contents

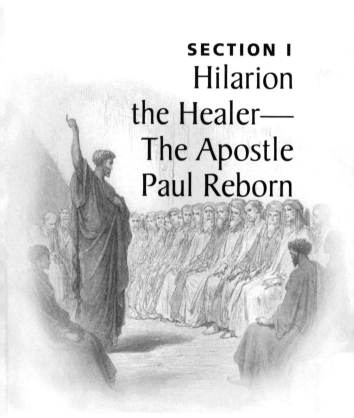

Who Are the
Ascended Masters?

*T*he ascended masters are our elder brothers and sisters on the spiritual path. Having balanced their karma and fulfilled their unique mission, they have graduated from earth's schoolroom and ascended back to God in the ritual known as the ascension.

These masters are a part of a vast brotherhood of spiritual beings and angelic hosts who work with mankind for the betterment of life on earth. The Great White Brotherhood is spoken of in chapter seven of the Book of Revelation as the great multitude of saints "clothed with white robes" who stand before the throne of God. (White refers not to race, but to the white light that is seen in the aura of the saints.)

These enlightened teachers have emerged from

all races and nationalities, from all walks of life and all religions. Many are familiar to us, having walked among us throughout the ages. Others are ancient beings of light, unrecorded in human history, whose names have long ago become secondary to the flames they bear. Whatever their origin in the vastness of our Father's universe, they all share a common light—a light they desire to share with mankind who are seeking the Truth they bear.

Among these saints are Gautama Buddha, Maitreya, Jesus Christ, Saint Germain, Moses, Melchizedek, Mother Mary, Saint Francis, Kuan Yin—and unnumbered and unnamed loving hearts, servants of humanity who have returned to the heart of God.

This Brotherhood works with earnest seekers and public servants of every race, religion and walk of life to assist humanity in their forward evolution. ⚜

Who Is the Master Hilarion?

*H*ilarion is a master of healing and truth—he serves on the fifth of the seven rays of God. When we come into the knowledge of the ascended masters, we come into an awareness of defining the path back to the Source, and we find that it can be walked over seven rays of the Christ consciousness that emerge from the white light.

The Seven Rainbow Rays

The seven color rays are the natural division of the pure white light emanating from the heart of God as it descends through the prism of manifestation. These are the subdivisions of the wholeness of Christ. The seven rays are outlined as follows:

(1) Blue—power and faith

(2) Yellow—wisdom and illumination

(3) Pink—love and beauty

(4) White—ascendancy and purity

(5) Green—science, healing and supply

(6) Purple and gold—ministration and service

(7) Violet—transmutation and diplomacy

Regardless of their color, all of the flames have a white-fire core of purity, which embodies all of the attributes of God and which may be invoked by those who desire to expand the Christ consciousness.

The seven rays present seven paths to individual or personal Christhood. Seven masters have mastered identity by walking these paths, defined as the seven archetypes of Christhood. These seven masters are called the chohans of the rays, which means lords of the rays. (*Chohan* is a Sanskrit term for "lord.") To be a chohan on one of the seven rays means that through this master that energy of the Christ and of God flows to mankind, to all who are evolving on that particular path.

The chohans are the closest ascended masters

to those who would be chelas, or students, of the real gurus. The chohans function in planes of perfection, but these planes are simultaneously one with the Matter plane where we are. And so we can say that the chohans are here with us. There is a congruency of Spirit and Matter where we are, and we understand that time and space are but coordinates of infinity.

All of the chohans are teachers of mankind. Each of them opens a path of discipline that corresponds to the ray and chakra (spiritual center) that the master represents.

Chohan of the Fifth Ray

Hilarion is the chohan of the fifth ray of healing, wholeness, precipitation and Truth. This is the ray of green, which imbues all life with the perfect blend of the blue and the yellow—the faith and wisdom of God in nature. The eternal newness of the color green charges man with the fire of the sun and the fire of the power to create. The healing green restores man to the primal nature of God. The ray of green supplies man with every lack and is the color of abundance and supply.

This is the ray of doctors, scientists, healers, musicians, mathematicians and those consecrated to Truth in all its forms. Hilarion works with all of these, and he can assist us in drawing down the abundance that we need to fulfill our mission in life. He also assists us in developing truth or clarity in spiritual vision.

Crown Chakra

Third-Eye Chakra

Raphael and Mother Mary are the archangel and archeia, and Cyclopea and Virginia are the Elohim of the fifth ray, which is also called the emerald ray.

Throat Chakra

The Third-Eye Chakra

The third eye is the spiritual center or chakra associated with the fifth ray of healing and wholeness. It is located in the center of the forehead. Here we experience God as concentration as we focus and visualize through the mind's eye.

Heart Chakra

Solar-Plexus Chakra

Seat-of-the-Soul Chakra

This is the chakra connected with vision, both spiritual and physical.

Base-of-the-Spine Chakra

Through it we are intended to see God's creation as he sees it—pure and perfect. Through the right use of this power of vision, we can bring forth the best in ourselves and in others.

The prophet Ezekiel described the chakras as wheels within wheels. In the East, the chakras are called lotuses because when viewed from the spiritual realm, they appear as a flower unfolding. Each chakra has a certain color and a certain number of petals that establishes its frequency or vibration. The third-eye chakra is emerald green and has ninety-six petals.

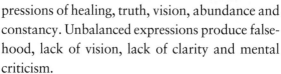

Rightfully used the energy of this spiritual center will bring forth the positive expressions of healing, truth, vision, abundance and constancy. Unbalanced expressions produce falsehood, lack of vision, lack of clarity and mental criticism.

Hilarion is the master who works with us to perfect and master this spiritual center. ✤

Hilarion's Service on Earth

We know of several of Hilarion's lives, and in these we see a long history of service to the flame of Truth and healing.

High Priest on Atlantis

Hilarion was high priest of the Temple of Truth on Atlantis. A short time before the sinking of the continent, he transported the flame of Truth together with the artifacts of the Temple to Greece.

The focus of Truth that he established there became the focal point for the oracle of Delphi, where messengers of Truth served under the direction of Pallas Athena for hundreds of years, until black priests penetrated the Delphic order and perverted the Truth that had been brought forth. The Brotherhood then withdrew this service to embodied mankind, since people were unable to distinguish between Truth and error.

The Apostle Paul—Saul of Tarsus

Hilarion was later embodied as Saul of Tarsus, who became the apostle Paul after his encounter with Jesus on the road to Damascus.

Paul was a citizen of Cilicia (a Roman province of Asia Minor), a learned Jew brought up in Jerusalem at the feet of Gamaliel, who was a Pharisee of the council and a doctor of the law.

Paul was a persecutor of Christians and consented to the heartless stoning of Stephen recorded in the Book of Acts. However, though the mind of Saul was prejudiced against Christ (by hereditary and environmental factors that cannot permanently alter the soul's direction except she* give consent), the image of the apostle Paul, his fiery destiny, was already etched within his spirit.

The Book of Acts describes the turning point in Paul's life: "And as he journeyed, he came near

---

* Whether housed in a male or female body, the soul is the feminine complement of the masculine Spirit and is addressed by the pronouns *she* and *her*.

21

Damascus: and suddenly there shined round about him a light from heaven: and he fell to the earth, and heard a voice saying unto him, 'Saul, Saul, why persecutest thou me?'

The Conversion of St. Paul, by Gustave Doré

"And he said, 'Who art thou, Lord?' And the Lord said, 'I am Jesus whom thou persecutest: it is hard for thee to kick against the pricks.'

"And he trembling and astonished said, 'Lord, what wilt thou have me to do?' And the Lord said unto him, 'Arise, and go into the city, and it shall be told thee what thou must do.'… And he was three days without sight, and neither did eat nor drink."[1]

One of Jesus' disciples, Ananias, following the Lord's directions to the street called Straight, entered the house where Paul was staying "and putting his hands on him said, 'Brother Saul, the

Lord, even Jesus, that appeared unto thee in the way as thou camest, hath sent me that thou mightest receive thy sight and be filled with the Holy Ghost.' "[2]

By the act of this messenger, Paul had the immediate proof that the voice he had heard midst the blinding light was none other than that of Jesus himself. Thus, it is recorded that through the Lord's instrument, Ananias, "immediately there fell from his eyes as it had been scales; and he received sight forthwith, and arose, and was baptized."[3]

In his own words Hilarion speaks of the great turning point in his life as Saul of Tarsus through the intercession of the Saviour: "That Great Doctor of the Law, the Lord himself, who appeared to me on the road to Damascus, allowed even me to experience that blindness that accrues from the dead ritual of the untempered zealot.

"He took away my blindness to the things of the Spirit. Ah, indeed I was blind to the light indwelling in his chosen disciples. So great had been the darkness in me that I must persecute that light that was about to swallow up the whole

... philosophy of Serpent and his seed. How my soul longed to be rescued, though I knew it not!

"Of the same measure that I fought with fury the light that would deliver me was my longing to be free. It was a question of polarization. And when men are polarized to the anti-Christ position, if they be truly of God and of Christ who is All and in all—though they deny him, yet by his Holy Spirit he will repolarize them out of the deadness of their words and more words unto the Alpha and Omega of the living Word.

"Oh, how I love that Christ who is All and in all! O thou Great Deliverer of my soul, I walk the earth in the power of thy love seeking my instruments through whom I might convey that conversion of the Holy Ghost that came upon me in the encounter with my Lord.

"He chose me as an ensample. Yea, the tears yet stream upon my face when I think of my former estate, the proud Saul of Tarsus."[4]

Paul Retreats into the Arabian Desert

Following his conversion to Christ, Paul was taught by Jesus himself in preparation for his mission. We read in his letter to the Galatians—

and he stressed this—how he did not receive his knowledge of Christ's message from the other Christians of the day:

"The fact is, brothers, and I want you to realize this: the Good News I preached is not a human message that I was given by men, it is something I learned only through a revelation of Jesus Christ....

"God, who had specially chosen me while I was still in my mother's womb, called me through his grace and chose to reveal his Son in me, so that I might preach the Good News about him to the pagans. I did not stop to discuss this with any human being, nor did I go up to Jerusalem to see those who were already apostles before me, but I went off to Arabia at once and later went straight back from there to Damascus."[5]

Many have speculated as to what Paul did during his sojourn in the desert. Hilarion has explained that Jesus took him in his higher consciousness "with others into his retreat over the Holy Land and at Arabia. I have been there and learned of him. And this was my desert sojourn in meditation with him, taken up as I was in my finer bodies and trained directly heart to heart."[6]

Paul 's "Thorn in the Flesh"

On his return from Arabia, Paul began his mission of preaching the gospel. During these early years, he had a spiritual experience that left its mark on him for the rest of his life. He describes this in his second letter to the Corinthians:

"It is not expedient for me doubtless to glory. I will come to visions and revelations of the Lord.... And lest I should be exalted above measure through the abundance of the revelations, there was given to me a thorn in the flesh....

"For this thing I besought the Lord thrice, that it might depart from me. And he said unto me, 'My grace is sufficient for thee: for my strength is made perfect in weakness.' Most gladly therefore will I rather glory in my infirmities, that the power of Christ may rest upon me.

"Therefore I take pleasure in infirmities, in reproaches, in necessities, in persecutions, in distresses for Christ's sake: for when I am weak, then am I strong."[7]

Bible commentators have long speculated on what Paul's "thorn in the flesh" could be. Many believe it was an illness or physical disability. In any case, this infirmity was no sign of God's weakness, but it was the sign of our ever-present helplessness, lest we should think that by some attainment we are above any other, lest we should begin to rest upon innate powers instead of the innate power of the Almighty God.

In reality, we all have our "thorn in the flesh" that we have been given to bear in this life. It keeps us humble and it helps challenge us to rise to new levels of self-mastery.

Paul's Missionary Journeys

To what end was the conversion of this Saul of Tarsus? Clearly, it had to have been for a very special purpose that the Master Jesus personally undertook the tutoring of Paul, whose experiences and writings in Christ dominate the New Testament.

In Truth, his mission was to build Christ's Church upon the Rock of his personal encounter with the Lord—to convert the "Gentiles," their leaders, and the children of light and to elucidate Christ's Person and Presence as the living Saviour in sermons and letters delivered throughout Asia Minor and the Mediterranean over a period of thirty years.

It was from the city of Antioch that Paul was called to the first of his missionary journeys, which took him through the southern part of Asia Minor. Paul performed miracles and preached the gospel, but the Jews were angered by his preaching; in Lystra he was stoned and left for dead by a mob.

Paul's second journey took him farther through Asia Minor and across the Aegean Sea, where he established Christianity's first foothold in Europe with the formation of a church in the Roman colony of Philippi in Macedonia.

This journey also took Paul to Athens, where he discoursed daily in the marketplace. Certain philosophers of the Epicurians and the Stoics called him a babbler because he spoke of Jesus and the resurrection. They took him to Mars' Hill, where the elders of the city met, so that they might hear from him concerning "this new

Paul Preaching in Athens

doctrine." Paul then gave a clear and elegant speech to the intellectual, erudite Athenians.

"Then Paul stood in the midst of Mars' hill, and said, 'Ye men of Athens, I perceive that in all things ye are too superstitious. For as I passed by, and beheld your devotions, I found an altar with this inscription, TO THE UNKNOWN GOD. Whom therefore ye ignorantly worship, him declare I unto you....

"'Forasmuch then as we are the offspring of God, we ought not to think that the Godhead is

29

like unto gold or silver, or stone, graven by art and man's device. And the times of this ignorance God winked at; but now commandeth all men every where to repent: because he hath appointed a day, in the which he will judge the world in righteousness by that man whom he hath ordained; whereof he hath given assurance unto all men, in that he hath raised him from the dead.'

"And when they heard of the resurrection of the dead, some mocked: and others said, 'We will hear thee again of this matter.' So Paul departed from among them."[8]

After leaving Athens, Paul spent a year and a half preaching in Corinth. Jesus appeared to him in a vision, saying, "Be not afraid, but speak, and hold not thy peace: for I am with thee, and no man shall set on thee to hurt thee: for I have much people in this city."[9] There was a great response to Paul's message here: "Many of the Corinthians hearing believed, and were baptized."[10]

Paul Imprisoned

Following his third missionary journey, Paul desired to return to Jerusalem to preach the gospel to the Jews, and he did so despite Jesus' warning to him not to go there. However, "The Jews which were of Asia, when they saw him in the temple, stirred up all the people, and laid hands on him, crying out, 'Men of Israel, help: This is the man, that teacheth all men every where against the people, and the law, and this place: and further brought Greeks also into the temple, and hath polluted this holy place.'"[11]

They caused an uproar in the city and would have killed Paul had he not been taken into custody by the Romans. When a conspiracy to kill him was exposed, Paul was sent to Caesarea, where Felix, the governor of Judea, imprisoned him for two years. Paul appealed his case to Caesar, and was therefore sent to Rome to stand trial.

The Taking Up of Serpents

In the midst of the journey to Rome, Paul's ship was overtaken by a great storm and shipwrecked on the island of Melita. Sanat Kumara describes Paul's experience there:

"Our story begins in the cold and rain by a kindled fire on the island of Melita midst the people who received the shipwrecked Paul and his

**Paul Shipwrecked,
by Gustave Doré**

companions with no little kindness. Paul himself had gathered a bundle of sticks and laid them on the fire; and there, out of the heat, came a viper and fastened on his hand.

"The barbarians, when they saw the venomous beast hanging on the hand of Paul, being superstitious, said among themselves, 'No doubt this man is a murderer whom, though he hath escaped the sea, yet vengeance suffereth not to live.'[12] But Paul, the beloved, empowered of the Holy Ghost, shook off the beast into the fire and felt no harm. And the barbarians, seeing no harm come to him, changed their minds and said that he was a god....

"And others in the island which had diseases came to the beloved apostle and were healed by the laying on of hands—because the Lord Jesus Christ and the angel of God stood by him....

"Now be of good cheer and be encouraged by

the great courage of those who have gone before you. Claim the mantle of the apostle Paul who awaits your coming on the east gate of the City Foursquare where he is the Lamb who is worthy to open the book that is reserved for the initiates of the fifth ray. Serving with the two witnesses, these witness unto the Truth, in order that the original lie of Serpent and all liars that have proceeded after him might be swallowed up by the rod of Moses, by the judgment of the Son of God, by the sacred fire of the Holy Ghost, and by the Light of the Woman clothed with the Sun."[13]

Paul finally arrived in Rome, where, according to church tradition, he died a martyr's death sometime during the reign of the emperor Nero (A.D. 54–68).

The Guru-Chela Relationship

Paul's direct and touching relationship with his Lord shows the intended friendship and personal initiatic path Jesus holds for every one of us—once we allow ourselves to be fully converted (the word means "turned around, transformed as a new creature in Christ") and subject unto the Universal Christ in life and death and eternity.

The Eastern term for the office Jesus held and still holds is *Guru,* meaning God-man, the dispeller of darkness—the incarnation of the Word (Avatar) who is Teacher, Initiator par excellence. The Eastern term for the office held by Paul is *chela*—servant of the God-man, devotee of the Light of Christ in the One Sent, the Living Master who wears the mantle of Guru.

We can gain many insights into the Guru-chela relationship by studying the life of Paul. We see that Jesus worked with him, talked with him. Jesus warned him, for instance, against going to Jerusalem.[14] Paul went anyway, got himself in trouble—Jesus rescued him again. It was a living interaction where the disciple heard his master but said, "Nevertheless, I want to do this." The master gave him his free will.

Paul learned by trial and error. The master allowed him to learn by his mistakes. He did not condemn him. It was a working relationship of compassion and love and growth, whereby Jesus desired Paul to put on the elements of his own Christhood.

Jesus, the Guru, has given us these insights

into the path of his chela, Paul: "Therefore, see to it also, in thy preparation for our calling, that you bring therefore a live coal, a lively coal of fire and fervor for the Truth as you understand it. For this was the quality of heart of Saul of Tarsus—believing what he had been taught, even a false teaching regarding Jesus Christ, my own name and my life and mission.

"Therefore, he persecuted my followers and, in them, persecuted my Presence. For I was in them, and my light was an offense to those who therefore enlisted Saul in their ways of exterminating, imprisoning, persecuting and torturing Christians.

"Blessed hearts, realize, then, that the fervent heart when hitched to the wrong star may be unhitched and redirected and therefore scale the heights of mastery, leaving behind those who seek to perfect themselves by the Law without the Spirit, who engage in rituals without love, and who are mechanistic in their judgments, very eager to point the gnarled and bony finger against any lightbearer for a single sin that they do think does soil the garment.

"Well, sin may or may not soil the garment. But the Holy Spirit is able. And that Holy Spirit in me did raise up Saul, and therefore he received upon himself that substance of his karma that created the state of blindness. And my instrument again, Ananias, therefore did pronounce that he should see by that Holy Spirit—and he did see.

"And Saul therefore became Paul and went forth as a chief apostle, one that I would send to the Gentiles. And yet he, being a Jew, determined to preach to the Jews, not realizing how infamous and how wicked was the core of their hatred and their rage against the living Christ. Thus, I came. Though he did not take my advice, so he loved me, and I comforted him and gave to him protection, even through the Romans.

"And you see, therefore, that God is no respecter of persons, and we of the ascended hosts may raise up friends of light where you know not."[15]

Hilarion's Remembrances of His Life as Paul

The ascended master Hilarion has given us some insights into his life and calling as Saint Paul: "Jesus the Christ we called him, and we were called of him as you are called this day. I recall the memories of his coming to me, empowering me with his Word.

"Yet first he humbled me on that road to Damascus, the humbling I sorely needed that I might bow to my own Christ flame that he revealed to me, as he also gave to me the key of meditation upon that flame that I might walk in his footsteps on the fifth ray of science and healing and apostleship and the preaching of the Word.

"Often I felt like the hands and the feet and the heart of Hercules, wrestling with the downward spirals of the earth with their atheism, their agnosticism, their intellectual pride and rancor against the prophets and the Holy One of God so recently come into our midst. Yet, all the while I remembered I was once counted among them. To have been once so proud and so deliberate against the will of God would forever burn in my memory the helplessness that we all have in essaying to be instruments of God.

"But the great empowering by the Word comes in the hour of the conversion. It is not the hour of the call, but the hour of the conversion when the soul answers with something that is deep. It is the flowing, it is the giving, it is that surrender when, as He said, 'It is hard for thee to kick against the pricks....'[16]

"My soul knew Him as of old and recalled to my outer mind the memory of the inner vow. It was not the first time I had seen the Lord Christ. I had seen him before taking incarnation, and yet I had to work through that pride, that karma on the fifth ray of much learning, much studying and superiority in social and intellectual standing that I had in regard to the early Christians. And so it was my own karma that was upon me whereby I was resisting the call."[17]

Paul Learns the Inner Mysteries

Through his epistles and his missionary journeys, Paul set up a rule and an order for the administration of the churches that he established. But he also taught to initiates the inner, sacred mysteries and a path of initiation.

During his time in Arabia, the apostle came as close as he could to the etheric retreat of Jesus and communed with Jesus, who gave to him the mysteries—mysteries that Paul said it was "not

Statue of Saint Paul at the Basilica of St. Paul's Outside the Walls, Rome, which was built on the site of Saint Paul's tomb

lawful for a man to utter."[18] Jesus gave him the inner keys to life—teachings that are being unveiled only today, teachings far ahead of his time, teachings that were a gnosis, or self-knowledge—the hidden wisdom of the inner Christ: "Christ in you, the hope of glory."[19]

Thus, by stages Paul put on the mantle of his Lord and accomplished His works as His instrument in healings, miracles, prophecies, preaching and fiery conversions. This was the true path Christ meant his apostles to walk—as the ascended master Hilarion once told us:

"If the light that is in thee be filled with the momentum of God and if the gears of the chakras be oiled with the holy oil of Gilead, then by the very vibration of your life you can intensify the currents of God, you can be one with God, you can be God incarnate as Jesus Christ was.

"This is what I learned from him as he became my inner and outer Guru. This is what I understood: that I, too, could become the Christ as the instrument of the Saviour—that where I walked he would walk, that where I stood he would heal, that where I spoke he would speak. This I learned, and yet I understood the unworthiness of the lesser self in the state of sin that is made worthy by grace, by transmutation, by fiery baptism and by the balancing of karma in service to Life."[20]

Another Life Is Required

Paul rendered a great service in that life, and he was one of those most influential in spreading

Jesus' message throughout the Roman world. However, before his conversion Paul had consented to the stoning of Saint Stephen (the first Christian martyr) and had actively persecuted and killed Christians. It is often the case that the taking of life in one incarnation requires another embodiment to balance that karma, or debt to life; and therefore Paul did not ascend at the conclusion of that life.

Thus Jesus, who raised up Paul to be his apostle, sponsored him in a final incarnation as Saint Hilarion (c. A.D. 290 to 372), the founder of monasticism in Palestine. His was the soul of Paul come again for his final incarnation to fulfill the law of balancing his karma incurred in the persecuting of Christians and the consenting to their death.

The ascended master Hilarion has explained why he was required to embody again before making his ascension: "Remember, then, that we, the apostles of Christ, did come under the dispensation of the Law that required one balance 100 percent of one's karma ere the soul enter the ascension in the light.[21] Thus, I was required to atone in my life as the apostle Paul and in my next life as Saint Hilarion for the sins I had committed before I received my Lord."[22]

Hilarion—Healer and People's Saint

In obedience to his Lord and out of love for His own, Hilarion once again accepted the gift of His mantle to teach and preach and heal. Thus, by grace, through the Lord's intercession, he settled his accounts with life and went above and beyond the call of karmic duty to bless untold thousands, the Lord working in him and through him.

Butler's Lives of the Saints tells of the humility and devotion of Saint Hilarion: "Being desirous to begin to serve God in perfect solitude,… he gave part of his goods to his brethren and the rest to the poor, reserving nothing for himself…. He retired into the desert…. He was a comely and even delicate youth, affected by the least excess of heat or cold, yet his clothing consisted only of a sackcloth shirt, a leather tunic which St. Antony gave him, and an ordinary short cloak….

"For years together his food was fifteen figs a day, which he never took till sunset. When he felt any temptation of the flesh he would say to his body, 'I will see to it, thou ass, that thou shalt not kick,' and then cut off part of his scanty meal....

"During the first years he had no other shelter than a little arbour, which he made of woven reeds and rushes. Afterwards he built himself a cell ... four feet broad and five in height, and a little longer than his body, like a tomb rather than a house. Soon he found that figs alone were insufficient to support life properly and permitted himself to eat as well vegetables, bread and oil. But advancing age was not allowed to lessen his austerities.

"St. Hilarion underwent many grievous trials. Sometimes his soul was covered with a dark cloud and his heart was dry and oppressed with bitter anguish; but the deafer Heaven seemed to his cries on such occasions, the more earnestly he persevered in prayer."[23]

Miracles and Healings

Hilarion spent twenty years in the desert in preparation for his mission and only then wrought his first miracle—God working through him, he cured a woman of barrenness enabling her to bring forth a son. From that day forward, he

Saint Hilarion, Abbot, by I. Romney

carried out a healing ministry.

He healed children of a fever by invoking the name of Jesus, cured paralysis and cast out many devils. Crowds would gather to be healed of diseases and unclean spirits. They followed him even into the most desolate and remote places. He tried many times to hide, but they always found him, compelling him to follow his true calling, for the love of Jesus.

Once, he sailed away and hid in Sicily, but

a devil cried out through a man in St. Peter's Church in Rome, "Hilarion the servant of Christ is hiding in Sicily. I will go and betray him." Still possessed of the demon, he set sail for Sicily and went directly to Hilarion; throwing himself down in front of his hut, he was cured. The saint couldn't hide from the people and he couldn't hide from the devils! As Jerome said of him, "A city set on an hill cannot be hid." Hilarion had become that city by his devotion to Christ, and by that devotion, he magnified the Lord.

Jerome, whose biography of the saint provides most of the information we know about him, records: "The frequency of his signs in Sicily drew to him sick people and religious men in multitudes; and one of the chief men was cured of dropsy the same day that he came, and offered Hilarion boundless gifts; but he obeyed the Saviour's saying, 'Freely ye have received; freely give.' "[24]

And then the Lord did something truly extraordinary through him. On the occasion of a great earthquake, when the sea was threatening to destroy the town, Hilarion turned back a tidal

St. Hilarion Castle, Cyprus, built during the 10th century on the mountain where the saint lived in a cave during his last years

wave. According to Jerome, "The sea broke its bounds; and, as if God was threatening another flood, or all was returning to primeval chaos, ships were carried up steep rocks and hung there."

The townsfolk, seeing these mountains of water coming towards the shore, ran and got Hilarion and, "as if they were leading him out to battle, stationed him on the shore. And when he had marked three signs of the cross upon the sand, and stretched out his hands against the waves, it is past belief to what a height the sea swelled, and stood up before him, and then, raging long, as if indignant at the barrier, fell back, little by little, into itself."

Toward the end of his life, the people's saint, for they had claimed him as their own, retreated to a spot in Cyprus so remote that he was convinced no one would find him there. It was even haunted—the people would be afraid to approach, he thought. But one who was paralyzed managed to drag himself there, found Hilarion, was cured and spread the word.

And so it was that the saint ended his days in that remote place, with many people coming to see him. After his passing, his followers buried him there, as was his desire, but within several months his closest disciple, Hesychius, secretly dug up his grave and carried his body off to Palestine.

The ascended master Hilarion has shared with us a revelation he received in this last physical incarnation on earth as the great healer and hermit: "I AM Hilarion! I have walked in the desert places! I have taken my refuge in the desert of life, but the multitudes came after me into the desert as I lived in my final incarnation as

Hilarion. They came for the healing fountain; they came for love. Though I would retreat, they would follow. And so the Lord told me that the gift of Truth and of healing is only for the sharing, only for the giving away."[25]

The Ascension in the Light

At the conclusion of his embodiment as the great healing saint, Hilarion, following in the footsteps of his Lord, ascended in the ritual that Jesus had demonstrated. He is now known as the ascended master Hilarion, ever accessible to his many disciples around the world.[26] ❧

The Mantle of Apostle

*H*ilarion calls us to walk in the footsteps of Paul, explaining that we are also called to be apostles of Christ. He explains that God will place the mantle of apostle upon us if we do our part:

"The instrument of hierarchy is a very tender instrument. And if you do not neglect the requirements of the service, you will find that God will come into you and live through you, and you will feel the broad shoulders and the robe of the apostle upon you. You will feel the mantle of Elijah and Elisha drop upon your shoulders.[27] You will hold your head high because you stand where the Lord stands."[28]

The life of Saint Paul is a tremendous example of the path of apostleship. We see how a single individual, one with the Lord and empowered by the Holy Spirit, can indeed change the world. Hilarion asks us to study the example of Paul and the apostles as part of our own preparation to be apostles of Jesus Christ. "Now then, beloved, you ought to know by heart the Book of Acts, chapter by chapter, for then you will know and believe that the acts of the apostles may be repeated by you today."[29]

Hilarion offers us his assistance and his mantle of apostle if we will take the first steps: "I bring that empowerment, beloved, for my heart has been kissed by my Saviour. And I am bonded to him, and I would assist you in the bonding of your souls to your Holy Christ Self through Jesus Christ.

"And I offer you my heart. I offer you my mantle. I offer you the staff of the Lord this day if you will but place yourself on that path of being tutored and God-taught, that you may indeed know the scriptures and impart them by the Holy Spirit....

"My beloved, it is this gospel of salvation that must be preached in every nation before the end shall come[30]—the end of opportunity for souls of light to be bonded to their Lord. Therefore understand that many have thought that it is the orthodox Christian message that had to be preached in every nation, but I tell you: it is the true mysteries of Jesus Christ that must be preached."[31]

"So I say, apostles of the Most High God, be on your way! It is the changing of forcefields, the changing of the boots that causes the quaking in the knees. I say be up and doing—left, right, left, right! Take another step! Go forward! You will find out what God would have you do. No need to sit and wonder. There is work, work in the action of the Holy Spirit. There is the joy of the service that is true brotherhood and true community.

"Find out what God would have you find out about yourself by immersing yourself in the great cosmic flow, the ongoing flow of service. Find out what the teaching is by living the teaching, and find out what we have for you at [our etheric retreat in] Crete as our assignment as representatives of Truth."[32] ✤

Pallas Athena and the Brotherhood of Truth

Hilarion has had a long association with the ascended lady master Pallas Athena. This great master is more than just a Grecian goddess of mythology—she is a tremendous being of light who ensouls the cosmic consciousness of Truth.

Pallas Athena's presence in the universe is the exaltation of the flame of living Truth. This truth she holds on behalf of the evolutions of earth as a member of the Karmic Board,* where she serves as the representative on the fifth ray of Truth, healing, supply and precipitation.

The flame of Truth is an intense bright emerald

---

* The Lords of Karma dispense justice to this system of worlds, adjudicating karma, mercy and judgment on behalf of every lifestream. All souls must pass before the Karmic Board before and after each incarnation on earth, receiving their assignment and karmic allotment for each lifetime beforehand and the review of their performance at its conclusion.

green. It combines the flaming blue power of God's

will and the brilliant golden illumination of the intelligence of God.

Pallas Athena ministers to mankind from the Temple of Truth above the island of Crete. Serving directly under Vesta, the Sun Goddess, she focuses the truth of God's love to the earth.

The Brotherhood of Truth

Twelve thousand years ago, a short time before the sinking of the Atlantean continent, Hilarion was bidden by God himself to transport the focus of that flame and the artifacts of the Temple of Truth to what is now Greece. The etheric Temple of Truth that we know today is located over the island of Crete where the ruins of the original Temple of Truth remain from the period when the island was a part of the mainland of Greece.

The ruins of the temple are just one more reminder that wherever light is raised and virtue is espoused, the hordes of darkness gather to destroy and to tear down, lest the flame rise above the mediocrity of their consciousness and consume it.

Subsequent to the rape of the Temple of Truth, the Delphic order under the Lady Vesta (first Goddess of Truth to the earth) and Pallas Athena directed the release of messages through embodied lifestreams serving at the oracle of Delphi. The wisdom released through them gave great assistance to those embodied who were keeping the flame of wisdom and truth on behalf of mankind. Eventually one member of the order betrayed their service, and so the dispensation was withdrawn.

Pallas Athena and the members of the Brotherhood sought to keep alive the inner mysteries of the retreats. The memories of the gods, the functions of the temple virgins and the oracles of Delphi were the last vestiges of communication from the ascended masters in the Greek culture. After the closing over of those sources due to the

Temple of Apollo, Delphi

discord and rebellion of the people, we begin to trace modern thought reaching and culminating in what manifests today as humanism.

The service of the Temple of Truth continues on the etheric plane, as Hilarion and Pallas Athena together direct the activities of the Brotherhood of Truth, angelic hosts serving on the fifth ray, and unascended lifestreams who come to the Temple of Truth in their finer bodies between embodiments and also during sleep.

The Brotherhood of Truth in Hilarion's retreat uses the flame of healing, science and constancy focused there. The Brothers work with doctors and scientists and assist them in their research. They, along with Hilarion, work also with those who have become disillusioned with life and religion and with their fellowmen who have misrepresented or misinterpreted the Truth, and thus they have become atheists, agnostics or skeptics.

The Brotherhood of Truth also sponsors all teachers of Truth, servants of God, religious leaders and missionaries, working steadfastly to draw their consciousness into a greater appreciation of the fullness of Truth. The Brotherhood also works tirelessly to introduce matrices of Truth into the consciousness of mankind wherever imperfection or error appears. They survey the scene in an attempt to find one or more contacts who will be receptive to the higher vibration of Truth that will draw the perfect plan, pattern or idea for a particular endeavor or service. ⚜

The Temple of Truth

The Temple of Truth is located in the etheric realm over the island of Crete. The ascended master Hilarion is the hierarch of the retreat, and Pallas Athena, the Goddess of Truth, is the Patroness.

The etheric temple is a replica of the physical focus built on the scale of the Parthenon. Long marble steps lead to the columned building decorated in gold frieze. The classrooms and council halls of the Temple of Truth are located in the immense area beneath the ascending marble steps. The hundred-foot altar in the center of the temple, a single beautifully carved pillar, holds the focus of the flame of Truth in a golden brazier.

The brothers and sisters who minister unto the flame and serve in this retreat form concentric

Hora Sfakion, Crete

squares at the base of the pillar. Their places are marked by mosaic designs, and between the innermost square and the pillar are mosaic patterns depicting great masters and cosmic beings who have served the cause of Truth throughout the ages.

The Flame of Truth

The flame of Truth enshrined at Hilarion's retreat is an intensely bright and fiery green, the color that compels precipitation, actualization, alchemy, practicality, healing and rejuvenation. The flaming blue of the power of God combines with the golden ray of the intelligence of God to focus the green flame of healing and scientific wholeness. The abstract, the ephemeral, the intangible, all are made concrete by the flame of Truth and the service rendered by all who are devoted to the life of God, of which it is a focus.

An Invitation to Attend Classes at the Temple of Truth

Hilarion invites us to attend classes in his retreat: "The dispensation of Hierarchy ... enables me to invite all who espouse the cause of Truth to come in their finer bodies to attend temple training and classes in Truth here at the isle of Crete, where the crystal ray merging with the emerald fires solidifies in the four lower bodies of man the blueprint of the City Foursquare, the geometry of the diamond-shining mind of God, and the cosmic cube that is the foundation of all spiritual building....

"When you come then to the Temple of Truth, be prepared for the reception of Lanello, our newly ascended Brother of Truth who by attainment wears the robe of our retreat and lectures in our halls, teaching and preaching as of old after the gospel of Jesus the Christ, who

Mark L. Prophet, now the ascended master Lanello

taught his disciples to become fishers of men.

"If you would be fishers of men, if you would carry the sword of Truth and wear our robe, then come and be initiated, and receive a just portion of the fires of Truth. For our God is a consuming fire, and he shall consume in this hour all that is allied with error and that defiles the image of the Holy Virgin."[33]

Souls come to the Temple of Truth in their finer bodies at night (during sleep) to be instructed in the fine points of cosmic law, the science of healing, mathematics, music, divine geometry and the laws of alchemy and precipitation. Many who come to society today with ingenious ways of opening the doors of higher understanding in these fields have studied under the masters in this retreat.

Soul Travel to the Temple of Truth

A simple request or prayer can enable the angels to take you to the masters' retreats while your body sleeps at night. Here is a sample prayer for safe travel to Hilarion's Temple of Truth over Crete:

Prayer for Soul Travel to the Temple of Truth

Father, into thy hands I commend my spirit.

Mighty I AM Presence and Holy Christ Self, I call to Archangel Michael and his legions of blue lightning angels to protect and transport my soul clothed in her finer bodies to the Temple of Truth over Crete this night.

Escort me, instruct me, guide and protect me as I work to set free all life on earth. I ask this be done in accordance with the holy will of God. ⚜

Hilarion's Role Today

*F*rom the Temple of Truth on the etheric plane near Crete, Hilarion works with doctors, scientists, healers, musicians, mathematicians and those consecrated to Truth who serve on the fifth ray, including those who work with all forms of media and communications. Together with the Brotherhood of Crete, Hilarion sponsors teachers of Truth, servants of God, religious leaders and missionaries, as well as those practicing the healing arts, scientists and engineers in all fields, mathematicians, musicians and those specializing in computer and space technology.

He, together with the fifth-ray masters, works steadfastly to draw their consciousness into a greater and greater appreciation of the full spectrum of Truth, which most have experienced only in part. To take them from a partial knowledge of Truth to self-awareness in the divine wholeness of Truth is the goal of these brothers, whose motto is "And ye shall know the truth and the truth shall make you free," i.e., whole.[34]

Hilarion helped to train Mary Baker Eddy, (1821–1910), the founder of Christian Science. With Jesus the Christ and Mother Mary, he commissioned Mary Baker Eddy to set forth certain revelations on the science of healing, which she published in *Science and Health with Key to the Scriptures.*

We can call to Hilarion and the Brotherhood of Crete for healing and wholeness, for the conversion of souls and for the exposure of Truth in the media.

Hilarion instructs us on the relationship between science and religion, both of which are aspects of the green ray of Truth, as he shares with us moments during his life as Saul of Tarsus and subsequently as the apostle Paul:

"Beloved ones, the lost chord of religion is the science of healing. Rebellion upon earth in the hearts of men has kept them from receiving the gift of this divine art. How well I know it, for I was a rebel myself, a rebel against the Christ, a rebel against his cause.

"How is it that those upon this dark star do rebel against the holy will of life pulsating within them? It is imperative that man give himself totally to the will of God in order to receive the gift of healing. And thus, as your beloved El Morya stressed unto you, the requirement is obedience to basic and simple precepts that you might advance thereby along the Path to receive the many gifts held for you in the heart of the Father, held for you by the Great Initiator, Lord Maitreya....

"Love is the fulfilling of the Law, beloved ones. Stop and think, then, that rebellion is a lack of love, a lack of understanding of the Father's love. For in love, all things become wedded to the divine idea, all fears and torments, doubts and despondencies melt. The fervent heat of love's transmutation brings all to the feet of the Christ, where in obedience they learn, then, to go forth as administrators of the healing ray.

"I was so blessed, beloved ones, to receive his

healing unguent that reversed in my world all currents and tides of rebellion, until by the blindness caused in me by my own rebellion, then, by the power of the light, I came to accept within a very short time the fullness of the mission of the Christ to every man and in every man. And so I became, by his grace, God-taught, and God revealed himself to me."[35]

"Onward, Christian Soldiers"

Each ascended master has a musical keynote, a piece of music that keys into the causal body or Electronic Presence of the master. Hilarion's musical keynote is "Onward, Christian Soldiers." This melody may be played to draw his radiance and the radiance of his retreat into one's world. Through this music, we can feel the same fervor and zeal today that enabled the apostle Paul two thousand years ago to inspire the early Christians to establish the Church of Christ in Asia Minor and eventually throughout the known world. ✢

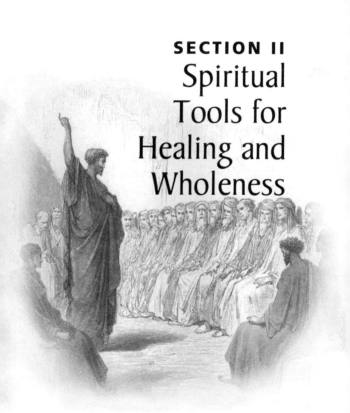

SECTION II
Spiritual Tools for Healing and Wholeness

The Healing of the Spirit

Often when people seek healing, they seek the healing of the physical body. But the masters of healing teach that when you become attached to matter, you will find that matter is an empty bowl, and unless fired with the flame of your heart, it cannot bring about the total spiritual healing you require.

Therefore, it is wise not to be satisfied with physical healing alone. Your soul needs healing far more than your body. The healing of the soul and the spirit is where you should first place your attention when you come to the healing master with requests for healing.

The healing of a portion of your soul will result in all things changing on the outer. Therefore, this should be the first prayer that you make and the first healing that you should desire.

Healing the Core Condition

Although healings can take place through medical science, the truth is that the scientific world knows neither the causes nor the cures of most diseases. Modern medicine uses drugs to alleviate the symptoms of disease, but most people are never truly healed of the core conditions, which they carry vibrationally in and about their spirit.

In actuality, one's spirit governs one's health. If the spirit is morose, the body will follow suit. And the morose spirit will magnetize other morose spirits, reinforcing the person's weakened state until a host of mental, emotional and finally physical diseases may result.

Conditions of the spirit are difficult to treat. In fact, they defy treatment. But if they are not treated, they can become a plague upon a man's house. Ultimately his only recourse will be exorcism by the Lord Jesus Christ or his saints.

If, for example, a person carries a spirit of anger left over from past lives, he must neutralize that spirit by invoking the power of Jesus Christ to come into his temple to bind and cast out that spirit.

Happy is the man who entertains a perpetual spirit of joy, for his spirit is like the sun shining at its zenith. He will know health, happiness and prosperity, and he will attract to himself, and forever entertain, spirits of joy.

The core condition of your spirit is focused in your etheric body. That core condition determines the vibrancy of your health and is the wellspring of your life. It is the source material you have to work with in the healing of your four lower bodies. You are not just your physical body, and in order to bring true healing to the physical body, you need to heal the etheric, mental and desire bodies—all of which leave their imprint on the physical body.

The apostle Paul gives us the key whereby every man may establish perpetual harmony in his spirit and thus in his core condition:

"Finally, brethren, whatsoever things are true, whatsoever things are honest, whatsoever things are just, whatsoever things are pure, whatsoever things are lovely, whatsoever things are of good report; if there be any virtue, and if there be any praise, think on these things."[1]

These are the words of everlasting life that spring from the fount of each one's being. Paul teaches us that by maintaining a perpetual positive mental and emotional attitude, we can be made whole through the Spirit of the Lord's harmony itself. There is no greater medicine than this.

Rising in Vibration

If your spirit has the determination to raise up your soul to the level of the Christ consciousness, all of the chemical elements of your being will "climb the ladder of the DNA chain" even as the fragments of your soul are climbing Jacob's ladder in their desire for wholeness. This process is a spiritual one. We examine it in metaphor, yet it is a reality that takes place within the etheric sheath as the components of spirit and soul reunite with the source of Being.

The goal is to raise up vibrationally every part and particle of your being as if you were using a spiritual tuning fork and drawing all elements of self to the plane of immortal being where they would resonate with the harmony of God. Going through these steps and stages of transcendence is a part of the ascension process.

The Need for Wholeness

Hilarion says, "Healing, beloved ones, is the integration of the whole man. You cannot heal in part and find the wholeness of the Christ. Recall how frequently the writers in the Gospel stated, 'And he was made whole.' Wholeness is a concept that is required as you pursue the knowledge of the healing arts. For healing is a science that must be mastered, and it is an art that must be skillfully practiced....

"It is wrong, beloved ones, to wait for some future time when you think by some miracle that suddenly, with one sweep, you shall step forth and speak the word of healing and at that moment you will be transformed into the magnification of the Christ. Healing comes as you apply yourself day by day to the invocation, the calling forth of the healing ray, the garnering of that ray in your aura and the chalice of your consciousness, and then the application of that ray as you are called upon in hour of crisis or need for one another.

"Another incorrect concept is that you are not in need of healing. You seem to be well, you seem to function, and therefore you think all is well. Precious ones, until the hour of wholeness, of cosmic integration, you are less than whole, and therefore, you require healing. Each and every one of you, each hour of the day, therefore, can practice the fiats of the Christ."[2]

Healing through the Rainbow Rays

Hilarion explains that healing is brought about by the light of God in its many manifestations: "The mighty science of alchemy is the science of divine healing. And that healing ray may be understood by you as the mighty tone of God—the tone of his symphony. As you extend the rod of power that is divine healing, you will be aware of that mighty chord within you—the chord that is the key to your victory.

"You will not be able to perceive or to have the power of that chord magnetized unto you until you have achieved the integration of the four lower bodies. For each of the notes of that mighty chord is played upon one of those four lower bodies. And therefore, if you perfect but one or but two, you will have only two notes of the chord. And without that mighty completeness of integration, you will not have the full power of the Christ to do his will.

"Therefore by purification, by transmutation, by consecration to the will of God, to illumination, you may have manifest within you the mighty rainbow rays of God, the sevenfold aspect of the flame and the two secret rays from the heart of Mighty Cosmos; for all are required for this cosmic integration. And therefore, you see why it is that the core of healing is the white-fire light, for it is the perfect balance of all the rays.

"Can you question, beloved ones, that the infusion of divine love within the heart of man brings about healing and solace and comfort? Can you question that illumination brings healing to the mind, to the outlook of man? Can you question that the will of God, when practiced and adhered to, does bring about healing? Can you question that the fires of transmutation, the ray of purity, the golden flame and the purple of service bring about an upliftment and a change in consciousness that is even outpictured in the physical form?

"Therefore you see that the rainbow rays of God give the balance in the seven chakras of man and key him to the mighty outpouring of the seven Elohim from whence comes this mighty tone into the chalice of man's consciousness. And therefore, it is not enough to reach to the heights of the green fires to bring about the transformation that will make you healers of men; but in science, in love and in purity, you must find all of God and bring his allness into the chalice of the present hour."[3] ⚜

The Divine Source of Healing

*T*he Chart of Your Divine Self is a portrait of you and of the God within you, which is the divine source of healing. It is a diagram of yourself and your potential to become who you really are. It is an outline of your spiritual anatomy.

The upper figure is your "I AM Presence," the Presence of God that is individualized in each one of us. It is your personalized "I AM THAT I AM." Your I AM Presence is surrounded by seven concentric spheres of spiritual energy that make up what is called your "causal body." The spheres of pulsating energy contain the record of the good works you have performed since your very first incarnation on earth. They are like your cosmic bank account.

The middle figure in the Chart represents the

The Chart of Your Divine Self

"Holy Christ Self," who is also called the Higher Self or the Higher Mental Body. You can think of your Holy Christ Self as your chief guardian angel and dearest friend, your inner teacher and voice of conscience.

Just as the I AM Presence is the Presence of God that is individualized for each of us, so the Holy Christ Self is the presence of the universal Christ individualized for each of us. "The Christ" is actually a title given to those who have attained oneness with their Higher Self, or Christ Self. That's why Jesus was called "Jesus, the Christ."

What the Chart shows is that each of us has a Higher Self, or "inner Christ," and that each of us is destined to become one with that Higher Self—whether we call it the Christ, the Buddha, the Tao or the Atman. This "Inner Christ" is what the Christian mystics sometimes refer to as the "inner man of the heart," and what the Upanishads mysteriously describe as a being the "size of a thumb" who "dwells deep within the heart."

We all have moments when we feel that connection with our Higher Self—when we are creative, loving, joyful. But there are other moments when we feel out of sync with our Higher Self—moments when we become angry, depressed, lost. What the spiritual path is all about is learning to sustain the connection to the higher part of ourselves so that we can make our greatest contribution to humanity.

The shaft of white light descending from the I AM Presence through the Holy Christ Self to the lower figure in the Chart is the crystal cord (sometimes called the silver cord). It is the "umbilical cord," the lifeline, that ties you to Spirit.

The Threefold Flame

Your crystal cord also nourishes that special, radiant flame of God that is ensconced in the secret chamber of your heart. It is called the threefold flame, or divine spark, because it is literally a spark of sacred fire that God has transmitted from his heart to yours. This flame is called "threefold" because it engenders the primary attributes of Spirit—power, wisdom and love.

The mystics of the world's religions have contacted the divine spark, describing it as the seed of divinity within. Buddhists, for instance, speak of the "germ of Buddhahood" that exists in every living being. In the Hindu tradition, the Katha Upanishad speaks of the "light of the Spirit" that is concealed in the "secret high place of the heart" of all beings.

The Threefold Flame

Likewise, the fourteenth-century Christian theologian and mystic Meister Eckhart teaches of the divine spark when he says, "God's seed is within us."

Hilarion stresses the need for the balancing of our threefold flame as a key to healing: "The mighty threefold flame, beloved ones, in perfect balance within you is the fullness of the manifestation of the healing Christ. And the rays of healing that flow forth each hour from Helios and Vesta and the ministers of Truth in my temple are yours and are all mankind's for the asking. For without the fullness of the Christ in equal manifestation of love, wisdom and power, you cannot hope to manifest the perfection of healing."[4]

81

The lower figure in the Chart of Your Divine Self represents you, the soul on the spiritual path, surrounded by the violet flame and the protective white light of God known as the tube of light. The soul is the living potential of God—the part of you that is mortal but that can become immortal.

The purpose of your soul's evolution on earth is to grow in self-mastery, balance your karma and fulfill your mission on earth so that you can return to the spiritual dimensions that are your real home. When your soul at last takes flight and ascends back to God and the heaven-world, you will become an "ascended" master, free from the rounds of karma and rebirth. The high-frequency energy of the violet flame can help you reach that goal more quickly.

Erect a Pillar of Fire Each Day

Hilarion urges you to take yourself up a notch in consciousness every day. Although you are in the flesh, in the body and in the world, yet you can be out of harm's way because you have daily erected the pillar of fire, the fiery coil.

The master says, "You must ascend over the

coils of that pillar of fire and secure yourself at the place in that spiral where you are out of harm's way, else you will constantly be a victim of the slings and arrows as well as the mudslinging directed against you.

"This is the way to be in the earth and not of it. It requires that each day you put on the whole armour of God, the full tube of light. As you give the 'Violet Fire and Tube of Light Decree' (see page 190) at least three times, visualize yourself in the center of that tube of light. It has no beginning or ending. It passes through the center of the earth and through the center of the heart of Helios and Vesta in the sun of this system of worlds. That mighty power of the tube of light accelerating, beloved, is your point of contact with your Holy Christ Self and your I AM Presence.

"Give this Tube of Light decree on behalf of every lightbearer and servant of God upon the earth and call to Archangel Michael to bind the forces of darkness that are on the increase."[5]

The tube of light is your seamless garment, descending around you like a waterfall of light, forming an armour of protection around you. It seals you from the mass consciousness and the energies of the world. As you give this decree, see yourself as the lower figure in the Chart of Your Divine Self, standing in the violet flame and sealed in this tube of light. ✤

The Alchemy of Healing

*H*ealing is alchemy. It is more than diet and fasting. It is more than herbs and homeopathy. It is alchemy. It is a sacred science. And it is a place where you learn to internalize the living flame in every cell.

All outer forms of healing are support systems, but beyond them there is the divine science. And we need to be careful not to have the false belief that any matter, from an aspirin to an herb, is the source of healing. It is only a substance through which the light can pass to us alchemically.

Jesus took the clay and his own spittle, made a poultice, and put it on a man's eye, and he was healed.[6] Was he healed by the clay? Was he healed by the spittle of Christ?

He was healed by the Alpha and the Omega of God that passed through both the clay and the spittle and restored this man's sight by an alchemy that Jesus knew and taught to his inner circle.

Ultimately it is the *light* that is the source of all healing. However, sometimes we find that the cells of the body do not have the ability to contain the light that could produce the healing. In such cases, the powerful presence of a healing angel, such as Archangel Raphael, can restore the capacity of the cell to respond to the life-force that is in everything natural around us, such as the water, the pure air, the food, the herbs, the substances, the homeopathic remedies—all these means we can use to facilitate our healing.

Through devotion to God and through our request, the angels can then come into our beings to trouble the waters,[7] to rearrange the molecules so that the cells of our being do not have any leaks but are intact and able to hold light.

The light of the spiritual fire must first heal the Matter vessel so that the Matter vessel can respond to the medication or herb or fast or whatever alchemy we are using. ❧

The Real Meaning of Disease

Hilarion brings the wisdom (wise dominion) of healing and the science of healing. He comes to teach us how to heal the diseases of the people of earth, how to heal their ignorance and their ignoring of those things that are being fed to the minds, the bodies and the souls of the children and all people.

Not surprisingly, the master has much to say about the origin of disease, which can be considered to be *dis-ease*, a state of the imbalance of energy at the level of the finer bodies of man—the etheric, the mental, emotional—and finally the physical body. For illness often begins not with the physical but with the finer bodies.

"My responsibility," Hilarion once told us, "is to release, through the fiery core of my heart, energies for healing, for science, for Truth, for the enlightenment of souls by the law of mathematics of the energy flow, the energy systems that can and will contribute to wholeness and the integration of souls with the life that is God here on the planet Earth."[8]

Speaking on behalf of the healing masters, Hilarion said, "There has never been a time in human history when mankind have been so plagued by disease of every form. Often these are diseases that are not perceptible to the people themselves, for they are the diseases of the mind, the diseases of character, diseases within the subconscious.

"This energy of malfunction, of disturbance, of an unnatural activity within the cells of the body of God on earth is reaching alarming proportions—in fact it is an alarm that has sounded across the cosmos itself. For if mankind be not whole, then how can they be overcomers in this age? How can they solve the larger problems on the world scene when their four lower bodies are so far from the center of Reality?

"We have seen, then, that Saint Germain and

El Morya

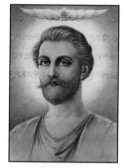

Saint Germain

Morya, masters of the age, require the support of the healing masters and of cosmic beings from many sectors of cosmos. We have seen that the dream of Morya to free the earth, that the fires of transmutation and freedom for the Aquarian age in the hand of Saint Germain cannot be realized unless mankind be made whole, unless there is a quickening.

"And therefore, we have appealed to the Holy Spirit, to the Maha Chohan. This noble one was summoned to our meeting by the Goddess of Liberty, the spokesman for the Karmic Board, and we placed the dilemma before the Maha Chohan. And he gave his reply, stating that he was aware of the proportions, and his concern was also a

The Maha Chohan

mounting one....

"His statement was that at the very foundation of the problem of disease, of sickness of every type was the estrangement of the soul from the flame of the Mother, the estrangement of the soul from the Spirit Most Holy. In the light of this assessment, he pointed out how troubling world conditions, manufactured to a large extent by the fallen ones, were specifically calculated to separate the soul from the security of the Divine Mother and from the energy flow of the Holy Spirit."

Sealing the Mind for Healing

Then Hilarion gave us an important key: "Will you remember, then, when all else fails, especially when you find that somehow there is a distortion in your mind, in your vision, in your ability to cope with life, that you instantaneously invoke in the name of Jesus the Christ the sealing of the mind with the dispensation of the emerald-teal ray?"[9]

Hilarion explained that this dispensation, when invoked, is performed by a special legion of angels assigned to the task who seal the mind and mental body in a forcefield of brilliant emerald-teal light, glowing now as green, now as an aspect of the hue of blue.

"Inasmuch as I am the chohan of the fifth ray, inasmuch as the chohans of the rays are the guardians of the Christ consciousness of their ray, it was given to me to organize legions of light for the protection of the Christ mind in the children of the light by the flame of Truth. Therefore, you may call upon this contingent of healing forces to reinforce the Christ consciousness and to saturate the minds of mankind with the healing flame.

"Know, then, that in answer to your call, I come forth with millions of angels and ascended hosts of light, some even newly ascended..., who have determined to join in this specific endeavor of locking the light of healing around the consciousness of mankind for the protection of that light, that Logos, that logic of the divine mind that it might mesh with the lower mental body, the brain, chakras and central nervous system, and be accessible to the race."[10]

Guarding the Mind and Spirit for the Health of the Body

Hilarion speaks often of the guarding of the mind as well as the spirit:

"In the matter of bodily health, the state of the mind and spirit must be considered. How foolish it is for men to ignore the content of the mind and to fail to examine that which they allow to fall into it; for the mind can be a pit and a snare because it is of the earth, earthy. Men should carefully watch the intake of their minds, for out of all that is absorbed therein are often compounded those animal-like qualities that later appear 'out of nowhere' to crush the evolving Christ consciousness, both in its infancy and as it approaches a mature perfection in the soul.

"A man must consider how he becomes his own worst enemy. Unless this be done, his progress may be slow; for within the circle of his being, he will find lurking the most crafty of enemies.

"There are many victims of maladies of the

mind and spirit who attribute to outside forces the distortions they themselves have taken into their worlds. Let us seek to cast out of each blessed monad the negativities that have entered there, in order that the eyes may see with singleness of vision the beauty of the emerging Christ."[11] ⚜

The Image of Wholeness

In Hilarion's love of healing and the healing arts, the flow of his thought is a never-ending stream of the panacea of peace men have sought but seldom found. Hilarion is living proof that the all-cure of God can be known, the elixir of youth imbibed and the sunbeam of Truth followed to its Source:

"O beloved ones, the healing ray is everywhere present. You cannot wander far upon this earth and not be in the presence of Life. And Life is healing. Life in its essence, when understood, always brings healing.

"There is no need for incompleteness; there is no need for a lack, for an incomplete manifestation in the four lower bodies, when Life is understood. Life with all the fullness of God himself comes to all each day in every breath, and the secrets of healing are themselves lodged within this divine pneuma.*

"Sometimes I wonder at mankind's lack of ingenuity in the discovery of the healing ray, for it is the most obvious of all of the seven rays, I think. I think, too, that in one another, in holding the balance of life for one's fellow man, the discovery of true healing may be known. For to see perfection in each one is to see the power of healing flood forth in all of its glory.

"Sometimes failure on the part of those who would heal comes because they have not held to the perfect image with enough tenacity, enough determination to hold a concept until the manifestation does appear. Mankind have trained themselves to wait for the springtime, to wait for the harvest, and they know it will come—to wait for the birth of a child. And the period of gestation of all forms of life is known unto them. And by scientific conclusion, they know that at a certain hour, a certain time, all will be fulfilled, all will appear in divine order.

* The Spirit, the breath of life.

"But when it comes to the unknown, there is hesitancy, there is doubt. And people wonder, How long must I wait to outpicture the perfect image? And because there is no precedent or set time for the full-blown image to appear, they become disturbed in their feelings, and they dash in pieces the matrix that divine love will surely fulfill in each one (in the cycles of time and space) as he holds to the immaculate design.

"For, there is no limit to that which you can outpicture by the power of love if you will hold intact within you the perfect design."[12]

The Immaculate Concept

The immaculate concept is defined as any pure thought held by one part of life for and on behalf of another part of life. It is the essential ingredient to true healing, in fact the essential ingredient for every alchemical experiment, without which it will not succeed. The ability to hold the image of the perfect pattern to be precipitated, to see the vision of a project complete, to draw a mental picture, to retain it and to fill it in with light and love and joy: these are keys to the science of the immaculate concept that Mother Mary and Saint Germain teach.

A certain understanding of this science has filtered through the metaphysical movements of the past century. The science of the immaculate concept is based on the realization that God has made man in his image and likeness; and therefore behind the outer manifestation, there is a perfect reality and a perfect form.

God is the supreme practitioner of the science of the immaculate concept. No matter how far man might wander from his individuality, God ever beholds man in the image of Reality in which he created him. We must have clearly in mind that the natural state of being is wholeness, is oneness with God, is the perfection of the Law. This perfection, this law, this being, is the True Self that exists behind the outer manifestation of an absence of wholeness. In reality, this is the Real Self that we would become.

This science of the immaculate concept is the law that is written in the inward parts of man, known by his very heart of hearts, yet dim in the memory of his outer mind. It is based on the visualization of a perfect idea that then becomes a magnet that attracts the creative energies of the Holy Spirit to his being to fulfill the pattern held in mind.

We can visualize the All-Seeing Eye of God superimposed over our third-eye chakra. Using the gift of God of clear seeing, we behold the perfect Master. We see before us Jesus the Christ. We have his image clearly in mind, as he is a key figure in our overcoming. Or we may visualize the Buddha or Kuan Yin or Mother Mary.

We translate the perfection of these sons and daughters of God to our own self, and in the calmness of our meditation upon God we know that this identity is also native to us. Then we begin to mentally affirm that perfection, even as we verbalize that perfection through the science of the spoken Word.

Having seen what you are in Spirit and what is the potential of your soul, you must retain that image of Reality in your thoughts and feelings. For the image is a natural repellent to all that opposes your Reality in manifestation, and the perfect idea becomes a magnet that attracts creative energies of the Holy Spirit to your being to fulfill the pattern held in the mind.

We can also practice this science for others. As we hold the image of healing and perfection for them, this becomes the matrix that the light can fill in to bring about healing, even while we fulfill the practical steps in the physical plane to assist in that healing. ❧

Karma and Healing

The most important thing about the healing path of the ascended masters is to realize that this is not merely a faith healing, although faith is always the foundation of science and the science of Being. But faith is a certain knowing and affirmation, an absolute conviction that God's Law does work and is efficacious in every healing area.

Upon that foundation, the masters have assembled disciples in all movements and around the world who say, "I am accountable this day. I see this problem in my being, and I want to get at the root of it. I want to root it out, and in the process of solving this problem, I want to earn my self-mastery. I want to understand the alchemy of being in command of forces of fire, air, water and earth, which correspond to my four lower bodies. I want to gain a spiritual victory for the freedom of my soul through this healing."

Therefore, when we come to the altar for healing and the transfer of light of the angels, we know we must bring something to the altar. The ancient Hebrews offered sacrifice, animal sacrifice. Jesus gave his life in sacrifice. What are we called to place upon the altar? The causes and conditions of our karma, that which is causative in preventing us from fulfilling our divine plan. It should be an easy sacrifice, shouldn't it? But it is not always easy.

Sometimes to attain spiritual mastery and physical healing, we also need to give up things like sugar, like nicotine, like alcohol, like marijuana, like a habit of irritability or anger or selfishness or envy or unkindness, ungivingness in which we stop the flow of life. The Law and the LORD both require of us something.

This is why fasting is such an effective means not only of physical changes and healing and cleansing, but also of spiritual enlightenment and a rapprochement with your own Holy Christ Self and I AM Presence. Fasting is a giving up of things we really don't want, like toxins and impurities. But it becomes a sacrifice because we get hungry and we desire to eat, which then becomes an initiation of willpower, and of understanding that God in us is the strength to meet our day.*

So we find that the exchange of our human consciousness and nonsense for divine light and wholeness—which should be the greatest bargain in cosmos—is often resisted by ourselves and loved ones whom we desire to help. So many follow after someone who simply requests a confession of faith through which there is, supposedly, an instantaneous healing.

Instantaneous Healing

This is not to say that instantaneous healings do not occur. However, there are many forms of instantaneous healing. One will come as in the way of Jesus, when Jesus himself takes on the karma of the person and bears that karma so that

* Some recommendations concerning fasting: Do not fast if you are pregnant or a nursing mother. If you have a medical or mental health condition, consult your doctor before fasting. Fasting for more than three days is not recommended unless you are under the care of a health professional with experience in this field.

he may be made whole. Then there is the situation where the individual has fully balanced the karma of that disease. It has no further inner cause, but has simply become a habit.

So the individual contacts the angel of the LORD or comes to the LORD's altar or prays at his own bedside, and he is delivered. This can occur because by prayer and faith and surrender of himself, he has established a figure-eight flow, an ascending and descending current from the I AM Presence to the lower figure in the Chart, who is you, seated where you are. That instantaneous healing is simply sealed by an instrument.

Archangel Raphael is a very powerful intercessor. Your Holy Christ Self is an intercessor. The messenger may be a facilitator, a conductor of light and healing currents. Your friend, your doctor, your health practitioner may be the same. Someone who loves you and takes care of you may be the one that brings about a very instantaneous restoration to wholeness.

Then there comes the faith healing where the karma is not balanced and the individual may not be able to retain the light, and in that instance the problem may by and by return. And then there is also the healing by hypnosis or self-hypnosis or similar practices.

So then, the violet flame when invoked daily by us begins to build a fountain around us as you see it pictured in the Chart of Your Divine Self (see page 78). This fountain of light, then, is called forth for the transmutation of karma, for the healing of disease, and for the healing of the planetary body. That service itself brings healing, because any service to every part of life accrues to one's own balance. The violet flame, then, is the means to securing permanent healing of the cause and core of a condition.

Karmic Causes of Disease

Pallas Athena is particularly concerned with diseases brought about specifically by the return factor of karma. Hilarion explains that "her committee of ascended hosts will assist mankind in dealing with their karma coalescing in the four lower bodies. They will assist with inner instruction, with a dispensation for the taking of souls so afflicted to the healing temples while their bodies sleep, to the Hall of Records where they will be shown, by the Keeper of the Scrolls and the angels of record, past performances that have resulted in present conditions.

"Souls ... will then be shown the manipulation of cosmic energies, the use of the healing ray. They will be introduced to Kuan Yin, the bodhisattva of mercy. They will be shown how that karma can be set aside and how they can work out that karma by service, by invocation, by communion with the Holy Spirit and the Cosmic Virgin....

"Where you perceive, then, karma closing in upon yourself, upon loved ones—the karma of age, decrepitude, senility, whatever the age, whatever the condition—remember to call upon Pallas Athena and the committee for the instruction concerning karmic causes of disease. And you will find a tremendous assist given to yourself as well as others. You will find a compassion developing within yourself and within them, and you will see what the ascended hosts can do for mankind."[13] ❧

Violet Flame for Healing

Hilarion has spoken of the use of the violet flame as a powerful adjunct to your healing of body, mind and spirit. But what is the violet flame and how does it work?

Just as a ray of sunlight passing through a prism is refracted into the seven colors of the rainbow, so spiritual light manifests as seven rays. The violet ray is the seventh of these rays. Each ray has a specific color, frequency and quality. When you invoke a ray in the name of God, it manifests as a "flame." You could compare this to a ray of sunlight that passes through a magnifying glass and creates a flame.

Each of the spiritual flames creates a specific positive action in the body, heart, mind and soul. The violet flame creates an action of mercy, justice, freedom and transmutation.

To transmute is to alter in form, appearance or nature, especially to change something into a higher form. The term was used by alchemists who attempted to transmute base metals into gold,

separating the "subtle" from the "gross" by means of heat. For both ancient and medieval alchemists, the real purpose of alchemical transmutation was spiritual transformation and the attainment of eternal life.

That is precisely what the violet flame can do for us. It consumes the elements of our karma, separating them from our native purity, so that we can realize the true gold of our Higher Self and achieve a lasting spiritual transformation.

In our physical world, violet light has the shortest wavelength and therefore the highest frequency in the visible spectrum. Thus, in one sense of the word, the violet light can be seen as a point of transition from the visible to the invisible, from one plane of being to the next.

The ascended master Saint Germain has sponsored the gift of the violet flame to mankind. We see the hand of Saint Germain in many aspects of this alchemy of healing. For it is indeed the Wonderman of Europe[14] who has advanced the cause of medical science and even pioneered drugs that increase longevity.

Saint Germain teaches that "the violet flame is the supreme antidote for physical problems." It has the ability to change physical conditions because, of all the rays, the violet is closest in vibratory action to the components of Matter. "The violet flame can combine with any molecule or molecular structure, any particle of Matter known or unknown, and any wave of light, electron or electricity." Wherever people give violet-flame decrees, "there you notice immediately an improvement in physical conditions."[15]

The following is a simple violet-flame decree (or mantra) that can be used to bring the action of this powerful energy into your world:

I AM a being of violet fire,
I AM the purity God desires!

The violet flame assists the healing process at all levels of our being. In some cases, the violet flame will take care of the complete healing of whatever condition you are dealing with. In other cases, the violet flame prepares the cell; then you have to do the practical work in Matter of the alchemy of stopping the taking in of toxins that compromise the cell again and prevent the cell from absorbing the light. And you also need to take the appropriate remedy that now will be able to transfer the healing because the light has been invoked.

This is a very progressive caduceus action of a yin and yang. Once you have achieved a certain physical, biochemical stability within the cells and organs, you have a capacity to hold greater light. Then the light comes down again and it builds an even greater chalice, and the new chalice can again absorb from the environment and from nature those things that increase health.

"More Violet Fire"

Hilarion has given his students a decree called "More Violet Fire." He calls it "my perpetual mantra, the unending river of violet flame." This mantra is known for its rhythm and for the spiraling action of the violet flame that follows the rhythm.

As you give this decree, commune with your I AM Presence. Feel the love of your "lovely God Presence" enfold you completely as you let go of all anger, worries, concerns and fears.

Visualize a waterfall of light descending from your I AM Presence. See this light being released through your chakras as streams of glistening energy going forth to bless and comfort those for whom you are praying.

See the violet flame dissolving the cause, effect, record and memory of your own and others' misdeeds. Don't forget to bring to the words of the decree your own special images of what you want the violet flame to accomplish. No problem is too insignificant or too big to tackle with the violet flame.

More Violet Fire
by Hilarion

Lovely God Presence, I AM in me,
Hear me now I do decree:
Bring to pass each blessing for which I call
Upon the Holy Christ Self of each and all.

Let violet fire of freedom roll
Round the world to make all whole;
Saturate the earth and its people, too,
With increasing Christ-radiance shining
     through.

I AM this action from God above,
Sustained by the hand of heaven's love,
Transmuting the causes of discord here,
Removing the cores so that none do fear.

I AM, I AM, I AM
The full power of freedom's love
Raising all earth to heaven above.
Violet fire now blazing bright,
In living beauty is God's own light

Which right now and forever
Sets the world, myself, and all life
Eternally free in ascended master
  perfection.
Almighty I AM! Almighty I AM!
  Almighty I AM!

Visualization Techniques

Decrees are an important tool for developing personal mastery. For example, you can use this decree to develop a facility for visualization by simply looking at the words and seeing those words that you are saying taking on the thoughtforms you image forth. See those mental pictures as cups being filled with violet flame by angels, masters and cosmic beings.

When you recite the line "Bring to pass each blessing for which I call upon the Holy Christ Self of each and all," see in your mind's eye a huge crowd of people. First, see the figure of Jesus Christ and the Holy Christ Self descending over one person. Hold that picture strong. Focus the lens of your inner eye on it. When it has become clear, you are ready to multiply your visualization.

Visualize a huge stadium filled with people—the bleachers in Yankee Stadium filled for the World Series. See the presence of Jesus Christ and the Holy Christ Self dropping over everyone in the stadium like a mantle of light.

You can add to your mental picture as many thoughtforms as you can hold steady. You can visualize the tube of light with the violet flame in the center around yourself and every single person in the stadium. You can visualize the I AM Presence above the entire crowd. You can see the blessings flowing from your seven chakras, from your hands.

As you master the words of the decree and then memorize them, you can close your eyes and see, with the full power of seeing that God gave you in the third eye, any blessing you want to see your violet-flame decrees accomplish.

Your mind should never be idle while you decree. When you know a decree by heart, close your eyes and begin doing your work for the planet. This is what the saints have called the mighty work of the ages. What you see, what you can conceive of because you know it is the Law of God, what you call forth, directing light rays through your chakras, you will precipitate; and it will come into manifestation on this planet.

Some have seen stupendous results from their prayers and affirmations. It is astounding how God takes our fiats and our commands and brings them about in his good time. Sometimes it takes years, but the hour of fulfillment does come, when it is the will of God.

When you give this decree, bring to those words your very special imagination, your special images that you want to see outpictured on the screen of life. God has given you a unique ability to image forth and to imprint your image on material substance.

No two people reading this book will come up with the identical visualization or thought-form. This is what enriches the kingdom of heaven—each individual sending forth the power of his mind, the power of his love, the power of his wisdom through the third-eye chakra to bring into manifestation the desirings of God and man, according to the will of God.

You can orchestrate a tremendous flow of light to the planet if you will just use this receiving-and-sending station that is your body. Therefore, do not allow any of the components of this receiving-and-sending station to be idle, to be not in gear, to be not focused, not aligned, not tethered, not concentrated. You must master your chakras and your four lower bodies if you would master yourself and your planet.

One way to assist in the visualization of the violet flame is to purchase a piece of violet satin or velvet to place on your altar. Another excellent way to see and feel and even hear the violet flame is to see yourself seated before a blazing bonfire; color it violet in your imagination and see each flame turn violet, purple and pink; and then see yourself stepping into the sacred fire. You may also wish to visualize a sea of violet flame into which you plunge for the cleansing of your four lower bodies.

Transmutation by the Sacred Fire— Key to Healing

In the twenty-first century, the healing of the etheric, the mental and the desire bodies of the race will be a far greater challenge to modern science than even the healing of the physical body.

Without the Holy Spirit's intervention and a spiritualization of consciousness among practitioners of mental health, the current practices of psychiatry and psychology will not be able to restore wholeness within the finer bodies of man, and this absence of wholeness will be reflected in the physical body.

Transmutation by the sacred fire—and specifically by the violet flame, the seventh ray aspect of the Holy Spirit—will provide the keys to healing in the Aquarian age. Those who accept this method of self-healing and practice it daily will achieve a certain level of wholeness even while they transmute much of their karma.

Those who do not accept this method of self-healing, and therefore do not practice it, will not achieve a certain level of wholeness and will not transmute that karma. The Law is the Law, and it is exact and exacting.

The Flame of Freedom

"Always remember that exposure to the divine flames can never harm or alter any part of your being that is a manifestation of universal perfection," Saint Germain tells us. "Just as mankind who are wise seek a catharsis in their physical as well as their emotional body to purge them from residual substance, so it is essential that they purify their entire consciousness through calling into action the blessed violet flame that focuses the forgiving, transmuting power of God."[16] The violet flame cannot hurt you. It can only consume the darkness residual in your body and in the world order.

The music of the flame of freedom was released by Saint Germain more than a century ago in Europe through the three-quarter time of the waltz rhythm of Johann Strauss. So, put on a recording of the *Blue Danube,* the *Emperor's Waltz* or *Tales of the Vienna Woods,* and as El Morya says, "Let your house be a house of light! Let your aura be filled with the joyous fires of freedom! Roll out the violet carpet, and see how the masters will come to teach you and to lead you in the paths of righteousness for His name's sake."[17]

You'll never know until you TRY. ⚜

The Healing Flames of Mercy and Forgiveness

An often overlooked key to healing is the power of forgiveness. Hilarion says, "Have you ever considered that you have the power to forgive yourself, in the name of Almighty God, of those sins that have brought about the condition that we shall term less than whole?

"Beloved ones, forgiveness is the beginning of healing. For the mighty healing ray of God descending to the chalice of the consciousness of the disciple stops as it comes in contact with human effluvia and densities."[18]

The concept of forgiveness as a key to healing was delivered to us by Jesus Christ. When he went to heal, he often said, "Thy sins be forgiven thee."

What happened? An arc of light, an intense momentum of his causal body, transferred through his chakras to the one who lacked wholeness, the one who was therefore dis-eased. That energy restored the balance of energies of Alpha-Omega, therefore eliminating the cause behind the effect that was the disease, and wholeness manifested instantaneously.

Jesus made the point, "It doesn't matter whether I say, 'Rise, take up thy bed and walk,' or 'Thy sins be forgiven thee.'"[19] It's the same law. It's the same principle.

Jesus also demonstrated the importance of forgiveness when he was on the cross and said "Father, forgive them, for they know not what they do." If our Lord and Master spoke these words in his time of greatest trial, how much more should each one of us imitate him in the daily testing of life.

The Price of Nonforgiveness

We pay a big price when we do not forgive ourselves and others. We pay the price in our bodies with a lack of peace, a dis-ease in our mental and emotional world, that often leads to physical disease itself.

We pay an even bigger price spiritually with longer lasting effects that can remain unseen for some time. Eventually they manifest in some form or another, even if we cannot trace them back to nonforgiveness.

A sense of guilt and a feeling of self-condemnation often stand in the way of the acceptance of our healing. God has already forgiven us, but many people find it extremely difficult to forgive themselves and continually revolve in their minds their shortcomings and errors.

An excellent way to clear away all this debris that is burdening us is to call upon the law of forgiveness and see the mercy flame—a flame of pink violet—sweep through every cell and atom of our body, and then just gratefully accept God's mercy and his grace. Invocations to the violet flame can remove centuries of accumulated wrongs that have been stored up in the subconscious.

The Violet Flame Is the Flame of Forgiveness and Mercy

This beautiful, blazing, singing flame is truly the wine of forgiveness, the wine of the Holy Spirit. If we will visualize ourselves standing in this sphere of violet light and feel that violet flame passing through all of our consciousness—our mind, our feelings, our emotions—this is the way to undo psychological problems, hang-ups, depressions, records of the past.

When Shakespeare wrote "The quality of mercy is not strain'd, / It droppeth as the gentle rain from heaven / Upon the place beneath. It is twice bless'd: / It blesseth him that gives and him that takes," he was putting in the mouth of Portia a key to the alchemy of this seventh age.

The quality of mercy and the quality of forgiveness is the very power of alchemy that is in the violet flame. This flame, then, is like a cosmic eraser. When we invoke the flame of mercy as the Holy Spirit, it actually erases the effects, the memory and the cause of sin in our lives. To the Easterner, this would be the balancing of karma.

There is no need to go through hypnosis or regression, for when we call upon this action of the Holy Spirit, all our fears, hatreds, resentments, rebellions are dissolved in the flame, and we are restored to the newness of the Christ mind.

Complete surrender to the will of God for

one's life can often bring the desired healing into manifestation. Just the acceptance of the words of the Christ, "Not my will but thine be done, Father,"[20] can bring peace to one's world.

The Strongest Power in the Universe

The ascended lady master Kuan Yin serves on the Karmic Board and many times pleads before that august body for additional dispensations of mercy for earth. She is known and loved as the Goddess of Mercy in both East and West, and she has kept the flame of mercy for the people of China and of every nation and continent.

She tells us that "mercy is the quality of love that smoothens the rough places of life, that heals the sores of the etheric body, that mends the cleavages of mind and feelings, that clears away the debris of sin and the sense of struggle before these manifest in the physical body as disease, decay, disintegration and death.

"Mercy is the strongest power in the universe, for it is the power of the will of God. The power of mercy is the intensity of love that will dissolve all fear, all doubt, all recalcitrance and rebellion within the race. The mercy of the Law is sometimes very stern, but it is always patient, always tolerant, and it sees the flame within the heart rising to meet the Christ."[21]

She reminds us that, "When you feel the need of greater strength, of illumination, of greater purity and healing, remember that all of these qualities come to you from the heart of God by the power of the flame of mercy itself. For in forgiveness there comes renewed

Kuan Yin

opportunity to fulfill the Law, and without forgiveness little progress can be made."[22] Therefore, in order to reenter the walk with God, we need forgiveness.

We have a need for confession, a need to tell God what we have done that is not in keeping with his Law. Until we tell him about it and ask for his flame of forgiveness to pass through us, we have that sense of guilt, fear, shame and above all a separation from him.

Today this is manifest in all kinds of mental and emotional diseases, split personalities, hatred of father and mother, hatred of children, and many other problems to which modern society has fallen prey. The path back to the Guru, the inner Christ, is calling upon the law of forgiveness.

Forgiveness is not something we need to invoke only for ourselves; we need to invoke it for every part of life—all who have ever wronged us, all whom we have ever wronged. Saint Germain teaches us that when we invoke forgiveness, it must be by a very intense love in our heart. We need to let each other know that we forgive and that we are asking for forgiveness. And it's a point of humility to say, "I've done wrong, and I ask you and God to forgive me."

When we invoke the law of forgiveness, it bursts like fireworks in the aura as violet, purple and pink, dissolving unpleasant conditions in our world. It begins to intensify until great spheres of energy are going forth from our heart and inundating the world.

You may visualize a loved one, a child, a self-styled enemy, a political figure; you may visualize an entire city, the government, the whole nation or the planet within this brilliant sphere of mercy's flame, becoming the recipient of waves and waves of this wine of forgiveness.

Forgive, and Be Forgiven

If you expect forgiveness, then you must be ready to forgive. "In small ways and in great ways, mankind are tested," Kuan Yin says. "And the bigotry that remains in the consciousness of some is also a lack of forgiveness. Those who cannot forgive their fellowmen because they do not think or worship as they do—these have the hardness of heart that encases the flame of love and also prevents the flow of wisdom." [23]

The mercy of the Law is like a two-way street. It is the signal that you send to God and the signal that he returns. A two-way street means a give-and-take with God. If you expect mercy from God, then you must give mercy to every part of life. The fulfillment of the law of mercy must be for the ultimate liberation of each and every soul. Thus, as we forgive life, life forgives us.

"The test of one's ability to forgive is a very important test," the lady master Kuan Yin tells us. "You are tested by God to see whether or not you can forgive yourself. And if you do not first forgive yourself, you cannot forgive others. Be gentle with yourself. Do not allow yourself to whip yourself. The flagellation practiced by some of the priests of the Church was in actuality the work of the devil. This is not penance. This austerity will only lead to spiritual pride and not to the attainment of the Christ mind.

"Be compassionate to the soul; be ruthless with the carnal mind. Cast it out as the invader of your consciousness. Be wise as serpents and harmless as doves. [24] Give no ear to the carnal mind—either a friend or a foe or a family member—but be compassionate with the soul who has not yet discerned the difference between the carnal mind and the Christ mind.

"And while you are tender and loving and merciful to the soul that is in the way of overcoming, be fearless in your denunciation of the carnal mind! Be the defender of the soul! Go into your closet and pray for the soul, and pray to

Archangel Michael

Michael the Archangel to bind those forces of darkness that prey upon the souls of the people."[25]

Kuan Yin reminds us of another facet of the flame of mercy as she says, "For many of you I have pleaded before the Lords of Karma for opportunity to embody, to be whole, to not have dealt to you in the physical the great karma of being maimed and blinded at birth that some of you have deserved. I have interceded with the flame of mercy on your behalf so that you could pursue in the freedom of a sound mind and body the light of the Law.

"Some who have been denied that mercy by the Lords of Karma are today in the institutions for the insane; for to them it was meted that they should experience the agony of the absence of the presence of the Christ mind, that they might know what it is to defile that mind, that they might return in a future life and appreciate the gift of

127

reason....

"You do not realize how much has hung in the balance of your own life because mercy's flame has been available to you. You have called and God has answered, and through my heart and my hands, mercy has flowed. I say this that you might have also the wisdom to understand that when mercy has been accorded you for a time, you are expected to deliver the fruits of mercy, following the works of the LORD and the way of wisdom." [26]

Forgiving and Forgetting

Time and time again we have all heard the cliché, "Let bygones be bygones. Forgive and forget!" This is so true, because if you can still resurrect the memory of a wrong that has been done to you, then you have not truly forgiven.

In order to forgive, the record and the memory must be dissolved from your consciousness. Kuan Yin tells us that if this is not the case, not only have you not truly forgiven, but "you have hardened your heart. You have stored the record as a squirrel with his nuts. Deep within the subconscious, deep in the etheric plane, you have stored the record of that wrong. You have not released it into the flame. You have not been willing to let go and let God be free to express through those who have wronged you, in those whom you have wronged."[27]

Forgive Seventy Times Seven

Kuan Yin has asked us to "understand the need to be pillars of mercy, to forgive seventy times seven,[28] to take the blessed children in your arms, to love them and love them and love them—and realize that adults, too, are children— and therefore, for the sake of mercy, to forsake envy and jealousy and strife and scorn and pride and prejudice and separation."[29]

If we can be as little children and pretend that it is Christmas today, we can avail ourselves of a dispensation she once offered us. She said, "Will you do something for me as I bring you the tide of mercy? Will you write your Christmas list as you would a letter to Santa, but write it to me and list all that you can remember whom you have failed to forgive or who have failed to forgive you, and give me that Christmas list? Give me also your heart flame with the authority to inundate life, specifically those whom you name, with an increment of mercy from my temple [at Peking] and from my altar."

She then asks us to start our "New Year" by forgiving ourselves all wrong, all infractions of the Great Law. The Goddess of Mercy asks, "Will you truly forgive, which is to forget, and to forsake the past?"[30]

Serapis Bey, the hierarch of the Ascension Temple, states the same principle in a slightly different way. He says, "In order to ascend, you must abandon your past to God."[31]

Kuan Yin sums up her entire teaching on mercy and forgiveness as she says very simply that our "hearts need to melt," for we need to forgive in order to be forgiven.

One of the best ways to accomplish this complete "forgiving and forgetting" is by the use of the science of the spoken Word, accompanied by visualization, in a mantra for forgiveness written by El Morya in his "Heart, Head, and Hand Decrees." ❧

Forgiveness

I AM forgiveness acting here,
Casting out all doubt and fear,
Setting men forever free
With wings of cosmic victory.

I AM calling in full power
For forgiveness every hour;
To all life in every place
I flood forth forgiving grace.

The Law of Forgiveness
Prayer and Affirmation

Beloved mighty victorious Presence of God, I AM in me, beloved Holy Christ Self, beloved Heavenly Father, beloved great Karmic Board, beloved Kuan Yin, Goddess of Mercy, beloved Lanello, the entire Spirit of the Great White Brotherhood and the World Mother, elemental life—fire, air, water and earth!

In the name and by the power of the Presence of God which I AM and by the magnetic power of the sacred fire vested in me, I call upon the law of forgiveness and the violet transmuting flame for each transgression of thy Law, each departure from thy sacred covenants.

Restore in me the Christ mind, forgive my wrongs and unjust ways, make me obedient to thy code, let me walk humbly with thee all my days.

In the name of the Father, the Mother, the Son and the Holy Spirit, I decree for all whom I have ever wronged and for all who have ever wronged me:

Violet fire,* enfold us! (3x)
Violet fire, hold us! (3x)
Violet fire, set us free! (3x)

I AM, I AM, I AM surrounded by
  a pillar of violet flame,*
I AM, I AM, I AM abounding in
  pure love for God's great name,
I AM, I AM, I AM complete
  by thy pattern of perfection so fair,
I AM, I AM, I AM God's radiant flame
  of love gently falling through the air.

Fall on us! (3x)
Blaze through us! (3x)
Saturate us! (3x)

And in full faith I consciously accept this manifest, manifest, manifest! (3x) right here and now with full power, eternally sustained, all-powerfully active, ever expanding and world enfolding until all are wholly ascended in the light and free!

Beloved I AM! Beloved I AM! Beloved I AM!

---

* "Mercy's flame" or "purple flame" may be substituted for "violet flame."

The Body Elemental

An often overlooked factor in healing is work with the body elemental. Since the day God formed your mortal body and breathed into you the breath of life, he assigned to you a body elemental as your unseen bodyguard and personal physician. This devoted servant has been your constant companion throughout all of your incarnations.

The body elemental is in charge of manifesting the divine blueprint for your body. Innocent and childlike, masterful and intelligent, your body elemental stands approximately three feet tall—almost an exact replica of you.

That body elemental is also given the responsibility of keeping your vital subconscious functions working in order: it governs respiration and the rate of the heart. As soon as there is a wound in the body, it immediately rushes in to close that wound and prevent infection. The antibodies flow into that area not purely by happenstance but by direction, because there is a vital intelligence within you that is a part of God.

The Body Elemental Takes Its Cues from You

Your body elemental takes its cues from you. It is a mimic of your moods and mandates. Whether you say, "I am well" or "I am sick," "I feel good" or "I feel bad," the body elemental is like a genie that will carry out your wish. Your karma is its only limitation.

That is why all the advice you hear about having a "positive mental attitude" is true. Whether or not you acknowledge the existence of your body elemental, your body elemental takes its orders from you and acts according to your will. All of your thoughts and feelings are transferred to it, and it immediately programs them into the cells of your body. So if you train your body elemental to think negatively, it will obey.

So often we set our own limitations. We

decide we must have so many hours of sleep, we can eat only certain foods, we can only do a specific type of work, we will catch a cold if we are in a draft, etc. These concepts can become accepted by our subconscious mind and can affect us more than we realize. They may be outpictured by our body elemental, which thinks it is obeying our wishes.

If we feel sickly, if we have concepts of chronic conditions, the body elemental begins to bear the weight of that consciousness and may even begin to stoop over. Some body elementals are actually hunchbacks because they are so weighted down by people's fears about their bodies.

Doubts and fears can paralyze our body elemental—people may have such great fears that they completely deprive their elemental of the opportunity to do its perfect work of healing and caring for the body. A positive attitude toward life can help it establish health and well-being.

Don't underestimate what your body elemental can do for you. Its knowledge of the workings of the body is far beyond the attainment of medical science today. It records the hour-by-hour status of every organ of the body and its systems.

So, if you appeal to your body elemental to heal your body, it will obey. The results, of course, depend on your state of mind and attitude as well as your willingness to follow a health regimen that suits your specific needs.

As part of your mastery of healing, don't forget to build a working relationship with your body elemental.

Overcoming Fear

We find, then, in giving our decrees and our prayers for the sick that one of our prime concerns is to see to it that the fears of the one who is sick are not transferred to the body elemental. We must be sure that the body elemental is sent the love of the Holy Spirit, that it is encircled with Astrea's circle and sword of blue flame,* and that it is enfolded in the violet flame so that it can perform its healing work without interference.

If we would have the full cooperation of the

---

* Astrea is an Elohim, a cosmic being, whose circle and sword of blue flame form a ring of protection. The intercession of Astrea may be invoked by using the decree to Astrea on page 195.

body elemental, we also need to invoke the fear-lessness flame—a flame of brilliant white fire tinged with green at the edges. According to our free will, we may allow this sacred fire to consume all our doubts, our fears, our anxieties, our super-stitions, our insecurities, even our fears or guilt that we are not worthy of healing and wholeness.

Fear and the acceptance of the mass con-sciousness is one of the greatest enemies of healing. The decree "Strip Us of All Doubt and Fear" (see page 193) is very helpful in every case of sickness, whether of yourself or of loved ones.

Doubt and fear attack the solar plexus, the place of the sun that governs the flow of energy in the emotional body. If your emotional body is quivering with fear, no energy will flow for healing. It's true of animals, it's true of children. If you get upset about a little child falling down, the child will get upset. If you tell the child everything's fine, the child gets up and runs along. The same is true with your body and your body elemental.

Hilarion tells us that "the body elemental jumps up and down for glee as followers of the greater light of God come into a knowledge whereby they might integrate themselves and find wholeness and greater reunion with the mighty I AM Presence."[32] ⚜

The Gift of Healing

While in embodiment, Hilarion had the gift of healing in abundant measure. The truly great healers of mankind, who can bring souls to the point of resolution and wholeness by a touch of the hand or a simple command, "Be thou made whole!" are sent from God.

The identifying mark of the true healer is that he walks in the shadow of his mighty I AM Presence, that he is humble before God and man and that he gives all glory to God for the works God performs through him, knowing that he is but the instrument of the Holy Spirit. These holy ones of God are self-effacing, and they will not necessarily tell you that they have the gift of healing.

In contrast to true healers like Hilarion, those

who set themselves up as healers but are not sent by the Holy Spirit are often puffed up. They rely not on God but on material means, proclaiming now this and now that formula to be the cure-all.

There is no such thing as a cure-all! For every disease of the mind or the heart or the soul or the body requires a particular formula for its resolution, its transmutation. And these formulas are often unique to the individual.

Nevertheless, while you wait upon the Lord, reciting your violet-flame decrees for the healing of body and soul, it is not wise to abandon those legitimate medicines and treatments that are helping you on the road to wholeness.

The Mantle of Healing

The mantle of healing has been given to Hilarion. A mantle is a cloak of light, a grid or a forcefield of light that is given to an individual who is sponsored by the Great White Brotherhood or by an ascended master. Worn at inner levels, the mantle contains specific keys that are a formula of light, hieroglyphs of the Spirit—a quality of light necessary to fulfill the office.

Hilarion is desirous of working with us for the action of healing, saying: "I come in the fullness of my presence as the apostle Paul and as the fourth-century healer Hilarion, who I was in my final incarnation. It was in that incarnation, beloved, that I balanced all my karma by applying the flame of healing.

"Wherever I went, I was called upon to heal, even to heal the wind and the wave and the conditions of the sea. Yes, beloved, there was nowhere that I could go, even out in the desert, where many would not follow me and pursue me and beg for healing.

"Blessed hearts, if you would have the mantle of healing, then ... enter in to the healing matrices fashioned into dynamic decrees and sing the hymns to Raphael and Mary whenever you can. Call for the healing of your minds and hearts and souls and for the purging of all that is less than the mighty power of Truth within you."[33]

The Gift of Healing Is Not Easily Given

The gift of healing is not easily given. If it were, we would know not one but many Christs in the earth who would walk in the footsteps of

Jesus. Yet even Jesus, when he returned to Nazareth, was rejected in the synagogue by his own countrymen, who said: "Whence hath this man this wisdom and these mighty works? Is not this the carpenter's son?"

The powers that be were offended by him. But Jesus said to them, "A prophet is not without honor, save in his own country and in his own house." Therefore it is written: "And he could there do no mighty work, save that he laid his hands upon a few sick folk and healed them. And he marveled because of their unbelief."[34]

You may desire to be healed or to be healers, but you may have lurking doubts and nonbelief in your ability to be healed or to be an instrument of God's healing. So, nonbelievers do not have the vessels of mind and heart whereby they might receive God's healing power and allow it to flow through them for the healing of others.

Yet, there is potentially far greater healing power flowing from your mighty I AM Presence through the chakras of your hands and through your heart chakra than modern science could deliver, using all the medicaments in the world. ⚜

The Flame of Living Truth

The flame of Truth is the dedication of Hilarion, Pallas Athena and the brotherhood of the Temple of Truth. Truth is the crying need of the hour. Truth, then, is born out of the Logos, out of the divine Word and logic itself. Truth is the geometry of Being, and the geometry of your divinity is indeed God. If you are not comfortable with the word *God* or with the concept of Deity, just remember that the pinnacle of your being is the geometry of divinity.

Therefore, this G-o-d is like a geode, for this is a rock that, when cleaved, does reveal crystalline substance. This is Nature's way of reminding you that in the heart and in the womb of the Cosmic Virgin there is an interlining of violet flame and crystal light. All the crystal substances in the earth are a reminder that some who have walked the path of Truth are indeed its embodiment universally.

The Denial of God

To a great extent, the denial of God by the agnostic is due to the soul's great disappointment in having been part of the various religions of the world and having been given false promises of heaven and salvation by the wolves in sheep's clothing.

For when these souls have passed from the screen of life, they have not been ushered into the courts of heaven but have been greeted by angels of record and by Jesus and the Lords of Karma, who have explained to them that they have not met the full requirements of the Law and therefore must incarnate once again. These souls have then become angry against their teachers, and when they incarnate again, they become agnostics because their disappointment in their teachers has caused them to become disillusioned with God.

Many atheists and agnostics are very devoted to a particular discipline, often the discipline of science. But they have not understood that science and religion are one. They have not understood that the God that is energy—that is the I AM THAT I AM, that is in the nucleus of the atom, which they would explore—is the same God who appeared in his Son Jesus Christ to Saul, who was himself a scientist and one trained in the law.

Often when agnostics understand the path of initiation, they become the greatest devotees. And this is why Hilarion, master of the fifth ray of science, is so concerned with working with atheists and agnostics. He understands that the real Truth of the path of Christhood has been withheld from them.

A Pathway to the Ascension

Hilarion teaches his disciples how to use the flame of living Truth to master oneself and one's daily life. It is a very practical application of the law that Christ taught.

The byword of those who serve on the fifth ray of science is "And ye shall know the truth, and the truth shall make you free."[35] Truth is a pathway to the ascension, and that path, known and fulfilled, does bring one to the place of becoming the embodiment of the flame of living Truth.

For Truth is a flame, a living flame that can be embraced and called forth. The following is a prayer to invoke the flame of living Truth.

Living Truth

O God of Truth, I AM in all,
For understanding now I call;
To see thee in thy fullness, Lord,
Behold, is living Truth adored.

I AM aware by reason pure
That only God can make secure
The lifetime's search for heaven's Law
That enters, filling hearts with awe.

Come now and help me Truth enshrine;
All understanding now is mine
Whene'er I open wide the door
No man can shut forevermore.

O blazing light of living Truth,
Thou fountainhead of lasting youth,
Come pour thy radiance through my mind
Until in peace at last I find

That God's own Spirit manifest
Is ever and alone the best
And holds each man in right secure
To understand the Law as pure;

That God's own Law is Truth alone,
For every error does atone,
And lifts all to the pure estate
Where Silent Watchers watch and wait

To vest ascended master youth
With blest Hilarion's ray of Truth.
Pallas Athena, thy Truth be
Our scepter of authority!

The Power of Conversion

Hilarion is especially concerned with helping atheists, agnostics, skeptics and others empirically centered who, often through no fault of their own but thanks to the "blind leaders of the blind" in Church and State, have become disillusioned with religion and life in general.

"The agnostics cry out today against the trivia of this age and quite frequently they take a stand for principles of the light," he says. "The atheists deny while the agnostics struggle to see. In our temple at Crete, we have determined to bring new meaning to life through the avenues of science and to stop the perpetual harassment of those forward-moving individuals who seek to assuage some measure of human grief"—even though they may not conform to some people's version of

Truth or science or religion.[36]

"My responsibility," Hilarion once told us, "is to release through the fiery core of my heart, energies for healing, for science, for Truth, for the enlightenment of souls by the law of mathematics of the energy flow, the energy systems that can and will contribute to wholeness and the integration of souls with the life that is God here on the planet Earth."[37]

As we might expect, Hilarion is an expert on the process and the power of conversion. After all, he himself was converted as Saul on the road to Damascus, when Christ appeared to him. Later, as the apostle Paul, he converted many to Christ. Of this time he offers the following insights:

"Truly I am called for the conversion of the world.... Truly it was a dispensation of the ascended master Jesus Christ moving with me and through me as his disciple and apostle and messenger for a quickened faith and a live and a moving religion whose witness was the power of conversion itself.

"And the miracle of his heart is yet the miracle of my own. And you will see the power of the apostle as the divine office that you may call forth from my heart. For this power of conversion is truly the sign of the presence of the Great White Brotherhood in your midst."[38] ⚜

Heaven on Earth

The ascended master Hilarion explains that one of our goals on the spiritual path is to seek to bring heaven to earth. As the apostle Paul, he knew the words of the master Jesus who taught his disciples to pray, "Thy kingdom come. Thy will be done on earth as it is in heaven."[39]

There is already a kingdom of light—a kingdom of "heaven"—on this planet in the etheric octave. The Temple of Truth is a part of this heavenly kingdom, and Hilarion has invited us to visit his retreat.

The more we know about the retreats and the etheric cities and what they look like, the more we remember of our experiences there, the more we can begin to outpicture them in our homes and work environment, in our cities and nations. As we create more heavenly environments for life on earth, eventually we will bring heaven to earth.

The master Hilarion says: "A place must be prepared on earth for the masters, for their coming and for the disciples attending their coming. As each home of light resembles more and more the etheric retreats of the Brotherhood, so there is the meeting of heaven and earth and there is the open door to the path of the ascension whereby worlds are transcended and the soul that is born in Matter is born again in Spirit.

"Thus, prepare the place, prepare the manger for the birth of the Christ, prepare the home where the eagles will gather together."[40] ❧

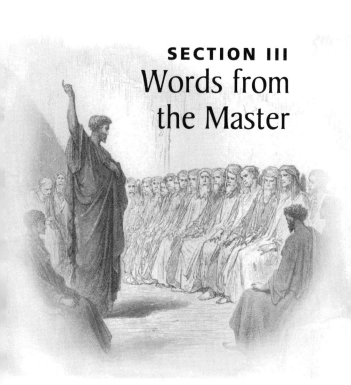

SECTION III
Words from
the Master

Hilarion Speaks

This section of the book contains one discourse given by the ascended master Hilarion through the messenger Elizabeth Clare Prophet.

God has always had messengers and prophets. For almost forty years, Elizabeth Prophet has been a messenger of God. Throughout her career, she has received messages from many saints and angels, East and West, whom we know as the ascended masters.

The dictation you are about to read contains the light and energy of the master. The words are his teaching, but they are also cups for the consciousness of the master. The spiral of light within the words is for your quickening and spiritual initiation. As you read the words, ask for the Presence of the master Hilarion to be with you and guide your understanding and help you to apply his teaching in your life. The Truth that he proclaims is vital to the times in which we live. ☙

The Gift of Divine Healing

And ye shall know the Truth, and the Truth shall make you free." "What is Truth?" Pontius Pilate of old put this question to the Christ. And still men are seeking to know the immortal flame of living Truth.

I bear it in his name. For I saw the unspeakable majesty of Truth, the immortal proof of the living Christ when he came to me upon the road to Damascus. So great was the power of that Truth that I was blinded until once again Truth's healing rays restored the sight to my eyes, the power of holy vision, through the All-Seeing Eye of God.

Few men realize that in the appearance of the Christ there was awakened in me the true inner vision of the third eye. And therefore, I went forth no more as Saul but as Paul, given the divine name by him who had fulfilled the Law in that flame of Truth.

The Inner Name

The inner name given unto me at that time signified the great power of the mission of healing that was to be mine. And so each one of you have the secret name that is given unto you at the hour that you accept your divine mission—in the name I AM.

Perverting this concept, those in the lower strata of human activity have sought to claim other names for themselves, thinking thereby to usurp the divine authority of the inner name.

Precious ones, it is not necessary that you know precisely the vibratory tone of your secret name, but that you know the name of Him who is able to bestow upon you every gift of purity and of healing.

Those who would enter in to an activity that is less than the mission of the Christ find when they assume other names than their given ones that they enter into a vibratory action not of the

Christ but of the psychic impostors who flatter and inspire them with pride and bid them to go forth in the calling of the lesser image.

Teachings on Healing Necessary to Your Path

I come to you this day to anoint you once again with the true calling of your immortal soul and to outline for you who have sought the mystery of healing some points of the Law that in your devotion you have neglected, becoming at times one-sided in your application.

I therefore bring you the tidings of great joy, the joy of the angels of healing who minister unto mankind and who bear witness to the immaculate concept, the perfect pattern held in the heart of the Father. For beloved Raphael who stands in the Presence of God perceives in his heart the immaculate design for every son of God upon the planet and those who are becoming sons of his heart.

If you would go forth to do the bidding of the healing angels, there is of necessity information that must be called to your attention. And therefore, I would give to you this day some of the meditations of my heart that I discovered and that were given unto me by the Lord Christ as I pursued the mission of calling forth those sons from Asia Minor and the Mediterranean countries. For I had many hours during my journeying to commune with Him and with the heart of the Holy Spirit and the divine one, Pallas Athena, the Goddess of Truth.

I sat, as it were, upon her knee and learned from the Mother of Truth those holy teachings that were also known to Mary and that she imparted, in part, to the disciples as they could bear them.

Healing Is Integration of the Whole Man

Healing, beloved ones, is integration of the whole man. You cannot heal in part and find the wholeness of the Christ. Recall how frequently the writers in the Gospel stated, "And he was made whole." Wholeness is a concept that is required as you pursue the knowledge of the healing arts. For healing is a science that must be mastered, and it is an art that must be skillfully practiced.

Those who have not the talent to design or to sketch from life upon paper must practice before they become proficient. Could any one of you here take up a pen and design the perfect form of the anatomy of man? You could if you studied and applied yourself, but you could not if you left your attempts to the mental world. And so it is with healing—the art must be practiced, the science must be mastered.

It is wrong, beloved ones, to wait for some future time when you think by some miracle that suddenly, with one sweep, you shall step forth and speak the word of healing and at that moment you will be transformed into the magnification of the Christ.

Healing comes as you apply yourself day by day to the invocation, the calling forth of the healing ray, the garnering of that ray in your aura and the chalice of your consciousness, and then the application of that ray as you are called upon in hour of crisis or need for one another.

Another incorrect concept is that you are not in need of healing. You seem to be well, you seem to function, and therefore you think all is well. Precious ones, until the hour of Wholeness, of cosmic integration, you are less than whole and therefore you require healing. Each and every one of you each hour of the day can therefore practice the fiats of the Christ.

Forgiveness Is the Beginning of Healing

Go back to the teachings of Christ. Study his words. Use the fiats that he used to make men whole. Often he said, "Thy sins be forgiven." He also stated that those disciples who would follow him would also be able to forgive sins in his name.

Have you ever considered that you have the power to forgive yourself, in the name of Almighty God, of those sins that have brought about the condition that we shall term less than whole? Beloved ones, forgiveness is the beginning of healing. For the mighty healing ray of God descending to the chalice of the consciousness of the disciple stops as it comes in contact with human effluvia and densities.

And so the way must be prepared. It must be cleared. You must go forth into the jungle of your own four lower bodies and cut down the path ere the Christ may walk on the palms, as on the Sunday before the resurrection, to receive the praise of the heart flames of all who are blessed to behold the perfection that he indeed is.

You see, beloved ones, you must make straight the way of the path of divine healing. For he shall come to you again upon the foal of an ass, riding and bearing the torch of your freedom. Will you be there to receive it? Are you prepared? Have you entered into communion with the Christ principles?

The Healing Ray First Enters the Mental Body

You must, therefore, realize that the ray of healing entering the heart of man first reaches the mental world. And therefore, the mental concepts of mankind must be purified by the immaculate concept of the immaculate heart of the Mother of the World.

You may, therefore, appeal to beloved Mary who herself, having received the early temple training, had prepared the way to receive within her own womb the manifestation of the healing Christ. Do you see the many years of preparation that went before her, working on the green ray to know Truth, to know the immaculate way ere she could be chosen to bear the one who carried the

165

Truth to this planet?

If you would have the blessings of the full-blown manifestation of the bloom of the Christ within your heart, you must first flush out the four lower bodies by this chemical ray, the green purity of God. And using with it the violet fire for transmutation, forgiveness, and purification, you will then come to the place where, having filled the mental world, this mighty green ray will purify the etheric records and patterns. And by the mighty power of the All-Seeing Eye of God focused within your aura, you will know the perfect design of your lifestream.

Now, precious ones, many among the student body have reached this attainment in part, and some have glimpsed it in hours of meditation upon Truth. And having purified their consciousness, they feel, "I am healed. I am whole." And they go about their business and their daily activities. But I say to you, precious ones, the service is only half performed when you have reached this facet of healing. You must now draw the power of healing into the seething vortices of your emotional world.

Clearing the Emotional Body

The emotional body must be imbued by the power of divine Truth. The reins must be drawn upon all misqualified energies, and that body that is the chalice of divine love must conform to Truth, must bear the pattern of pure love within you. And sometimes, because of the warring of the carnal mind and its influence over the emotions, there is a resistance to Truth. The resistance is actually in the residual substance of the subconscious world as it has magnetized the emotions of man.

And thus, mankind's energies are channeled in a certain direction, and these are grooves in his consciousness. And these grooves that have carried off the energies of God for generations must be filled in as men would fill in trenches. And sometimes this is a painful process, for it demands the rearrangement of the energies and the flow of light within the forcefield of your four lower bodies.

And therefore, there is war. And you find within your members one part in struggle against another. This I experienced in my life as Paul. And

167

yet always the magnet of the higher Truth, the polarization of my lifestream with the Great Central Sun was able to draw off the impurities, the residual substance of past embodiments, and I could go forth to see the Daystar of his appearing and the Truth descending into my forcefield.

The Healing of the Physical Body

When you have achieved a certain degree of polarization to the power of Truth within these three bodies, you will find that there is of necessity a great change that will also take place in the physical forcefield. But this change will not take place unless you determine to call it forth, unless you determine to draw down from those three levels of consciousness as well as from your Holy Christ Self all of the power and momentum of your God Presence and that which you have been able to glean and hold in the chalice of the physical form, which is intended to be the temple of the living God. For here in the now the lily of the Christ is intended to blossom forth, to be, and to hold forth the voice of Truth to a wayward generation.

Can you function without a physical form, precious ones? Aye, not in this octave. Would you be elsewhere? Perhaps, but your mission could not be fulfilled. And thus a return once again, another descent of your soul into physical form might be required should you pass off lightly the calling of your present position in the world arena.

Now, beloved ones, having a physical form partially dedicated to Truth and partially involved in the world of the senses is not as the ascended masters have intended that you should be, consecrated as you have been to the holy cause of freedom for this earth.

Therefore, think wisely and think well of that which you allow to inhabit the forcefield of your physical bodies. Think well upon the temple. Think well upon the science of God, the perfectionment of that temple, and meditate upon the holy precepts of God-purity for it.

The Power of the Spoken Word

I, Hilarion, have pledged myself this day to help you, each one, to use all the knowledge that you have garnered, and then to add some to it

that each one of you might become better representatives of the ascended masters to the mankind
of this planet.

I therefore would call to your attention the
words of the Christ, "Not that which goeth into
the mouth defileth a man; but that which cometh
out." The passageway of the mouth, the oracle of
God, is a key to salvation; for here the throat
chakra, the mighty power of God and of his will,
speaks forth the Word and can magnetize the
mighty power of the threefold flame to change
conditions across the face of the planet.

It is not only the knowledge of the Truth but
the speaking forth of the Word and the putting of
that Word into action that makes you men of the
hour and men for all seasons, as beloved El
Morya has of recent date been referred to.

Drink In the Holy Breath

Those who would do the will of God, then,
will think once, will think twice, and think again
at the power of holy integration that comes forth
from the flame of living Truth to bring into divine
consonance and harmony the four lower bodies of
man. Take heed, then, that your application be

not one-sided, that you do not favor one of these vehicles. For the sun does shine upon the race of mankind north, south, east, and west.

The four winds of the Holy Spirit do breathe forth now across the face of the earth in the four lower bodies of mankind and the four lower bodies of this planet. And in this mighty release of surging power, elemental life arises to meet the call and the need of the hour.

Beloved ones, as you arise in consciousness, drink in then, by the power of the holy breath from the heart of Alpha and Omega, this holy breath that shall rejuvenate and resurrect your own four lower bodies. And I am placing within each of your four lower bodies a talisman of my own flame of Truth, manifest as the emerald green cross, the flame of His Truth.

And by having focused within each of your four lower bodies the magnificent power of the purity of my ray, you will find that cosmic integration will be more and more apparent to you, and the science of how to perform and achieve this integration will be made known to your outer and inner consciousness.

Go Forth Bearing the Flame of Truth

Therefore, as you go forth bearing the mighty flame of Truth, remember that the physician must first heal himself before he can go forth to heal the multitudes, to multiply the bread and the fishes, to change the water into wine. The mighty science of alchemy is the science of divine healing. And that healing ray may be understood by you as the mighty tone of God—the tone of his symphony.

And as you extend the rod of power that is divine healing, you will be aware of that mighty chord within you—the chord that is the key to your victory. You will not be able to perceive or to have the power of that chord magnetized unto you until you have achieved the integration of the four lower bodies. For each of the notes of that mighty chord is played upon one of those four lower bodies.

And therefore, if you perfect but one or but two, you will have only two notes of the chord. And without that mighty completeness of integration, you will not have the full power of the Christ to do his will.

Therefore by purification, by transmutation,

by consecration to the will of God, to illumination, you may have manifest within you the mighty rainbow rays of God, the sevenfold aspect of the flame and the two secret rays from the heart of Mighty Cosmos; for all are required for this cosmic integration. And therefore, you see why it is that the core of healing is the white-fire light, for it is the perfect balance of all the rays.

Healing by the Rainbow Rays

Can you question, beloved ones, that the infusion of divine love within the heart of man brings about healing and solace and comfort? Can you question that illumination brings healing to the mind, to the outlook of man? Can you question that the will of God, when practiced and adhered to, does bring about healing? Can you question that the fires of transmutation, the ray of purity, the golden flame and the purple of service bring about an upliftment and a change in consciousness that is even outpictured in the physical form?

Therefore, you see that the rainbow rays of God give the balance in the seven chakras of man and key him to the mighty outpouring of the seven Elohim from whence comes this mighty tone into the chalice of man's consciousness. And therefore, it is not enough to reach to the heights of the green fires to bring about the transformation that will make of you healers of men, but in science, in love and in purity you must find all of God and bring his allness into the chalice of the present hour.

Dedication Is Necessary

To have bestowed upon you, then, the fullness of the cosmic momentum of divine healing during this hour of world crisis is indeed a great gift. The opportunity that has been given to you to be healers among men must be taken by you. It must be applied.

But most of all, you must find in your heart the dedication to that which you do not yet understand. And in dedication, even to the unknown God, you will find coming to be within your forcefield the understanding of the known God. And you will know him as he is, even as he is known to the hosts of light and the ascended masters.

But, precious ones, he who would have the gift of healing in the fullness of manifestation must realize that because it is comprised of the allness and completeness of God, he must offer himself completely unto God.

The scarcity of the true divine healers upon the planet in this hour is a testimony to the fact that most people who ask for the healing ray have not yet been willing to give their all to the Father-Mother principle of life. And although they have a deep love and devotion and compassion for their brethren, they have not yet relinquished personal desire, personal wants. And thus, some aspect of the sevenfold flames of God is wanting within their worlds. This, therefore, is the key to the mystery of the gift of healing.

He who would walk as a teacher among mankind might succeed to a great extent through the use of illumination's ray. And there are many offices and callings that can be achieved to a remarkable degree without total dedication, without the allness and wholeness of this complete cosmic integration.

But he who would actually carry within his hand the fire of God that transforms the brethren upon the planet at the touch and at the command must realize that here in the heart of the Temple of Truth those initiates who have applied to me to earn their ascension on the ray of divine healing have had to have embodiments where the allness and completeness of their lives was given in service.

Here we teach how man can live in the world of form and yet not be of that world—how man can go forth carrying the ray and the scepter of Truth with total integration, total dedication and the totality of his desire world focused upon the All-Seeing Eye that is the ray of healing focused within your form.

This Path Is Not Difficult

Beloved ones, this is not difficult. It requires most of all understanding that that which you give unto God in service is immediately given back to you—purified, transmuted and charged with the full power and momentum of God-victory.

You may not always receive the blessing in your outer consciousness, but each sacrifice, each gift that is laid upon the altar of God returns to your causal body of light a most magnificent gift and jewel that is the focus and ray that magnetizes more and more of his light.

And thereby, in giving all to God, you are polishing the star, the halo of your crown. And you see that at any hour in any day when you achieve the fullness of your gift to God, you may find that suddenly, swiftly like lightning and by the power of thunder and the holy wind of the Holy Spirit, you are then imbued with the power of wholeness.

Instantaneous Healing Is Testimony to Total Consecration

The transfiguration of the Christ was testimony to his complete dedication. And from that time forward he was among mankind a focus, an electrode of such magnificent power that all the earth trembled before his presence. And those who had separated themselves from God by condemnation or other sins against the Holy Spirit knew that in his presence the power to command life would be answered on the instant. Instantaneous healing, then, is testimony to total

177

consecration.

Beloved ones, the master key, then, is divine love. For in love all is understood as belonging to God in the first place. And you understand that in giving your all unto him you are one with him and have no need of any other source of supply, of entertainment or of delving into the intellectual curiosities that are popular in the present day and that always arise to tempt mankind away from that total givingness.

If God, therefore, gave his only begotten Son unto the world that through him the world might be saved, think you not that at any hour of the day he is ready to give unto you the scepter of power that is your own Holy Christ Self identity?

One With God Is a Majority

Exchange, then, the garments of the flesh, the tatters and tares of this world, for the seamless robe and watch how the world is changed with you. For healing in your forcefield means healing everywhere upon this planetary body. For as you are (as God is in you) the authority for this earth, you will find that in geometric proportion by the infinite calculus of the Spirit, one with God is a majority for the entire universe.

You see, then, that you are but a replica of this planetary body in your forcefield and in your four lower bodies. And as you have commanded the waves to be silent and still in your forms, so they are commanded on a world scale.

Thus, the Christ had the power to change the entire course of history. You also have that power resident within the Holy Christ Self of each one of you. In this very room the power of the Christ magnified, consecrated, intensified by devotion and service is enough to magnetize the earth to the victory of the golden age.

And when we say that mankind must be illumined ere we would hold back their karma, when we say that mankind must themselves accept the Christ in order to preserve this planetary body, we are saying that without illumined Christhood, the very atoms and cells of their four lower bodies can no longer hold together, for want of the cohesive power of divine love. And therefore, what happens on a world scale is the product of what is happening on an individual scale as men commit themselves to the darkness of insanity and give their bodies so freely to the lusts of the flesh.

But, precious ones, the power and the torch of that light and fire that you carry in your Christ Self has enough illumination and enough healing power that if it be lifted up as a light unto the world will draw all mankind unto the torch that is their Holy Christ Self and to their own identity that is the fullness of divine illumination and the will of God that will cause them to alter their course and take in hand the precepts of divine Law.

Therefore, not by interceding for their karma but by becoming the Christ you can achieve the staying of the karma of mankind. For in illumination is the transformation of the healing ray.

All is not lost, then, if you determine this day to consecrate yourselves to the power of Truth, to call to me and ask for the fire of my heart to assist you in that holy integration that you so require in this hour. For I come because many have asked, What more can we do to become more like thee, O God?

I Come with the Key

And so, I come with the answer and with the key. And if it be heeded and taken, you will find that the power of Truth, as it is released from the heart of the Great Central Sun Magnet, will "draw all men unto me." For I AM—the I AM of me is—the living Christ and I bear witness to Him who showed me along the way of life that the only Truth, the only Way, the only love and the only power is the victory of the momentum of God within the individual forcefield of all mankind.

Take up the cross, then, as I and so many others who followed Him have done. Take it up and realize that that cross is the symbol of your cosmic integration—each of the four bars (the four lower bodies) dedicated to the white-fire core of Alpha and Omega where God and man meet in perfect identity, in perfect union that shall make of you each one a mighty sovereign state, an inviolate arch (arc) of triumph for all the sons of men.

Give Yourselves to the Victory

You can see, beloved ones, that the victory is given unto those who give themselves to the victory. Therefore, take the victory today. Take it to your hearts and let this year be dedicated to the victory of light, to the victory of purity, to the mighty healing rays that we bear and that we are releasing every day throughout the year in each tiny leaf and plant as the chlorophyll ray transmits to the physical body all that is in store for man from the etheric levels and that which has been locked as matrices of power in the mental and emotional belts of this planet.

See, then, the salvation of God as ye are made whole by the threefold flame balanced in power, wisdom and love, attuned to the key and the mighty tone that is your cosmic identity.

Beloved ones, when you hear the name of God, the rushing of the mighty waters, the wind of the sacred fire, then shall ye know that the day is at hand for your mission to be accomplished.

Maintain the vigil of listening grace, then. Keep the vigil with Mother Mary. Keep it on behalf of the youth. For right within your own God potential there is the power that can restore this generation and bring men to the feet of the master Christ himself.

Faith Is Not Enough

It does not matter to us through what avenue these little ones are brought to his feet. It matters that they keep the precepts of the Law and that when they come to full maturity and adulthood they shall find that there is written upon this earth a body of knowledge, a compendium of the precepts of God's Law that will be magnetized in their hearts because they have first been consecrated and dedicated by your prayers and by their commitment.

Men may walk in faith for a time. They may walk and lean upon the rod of His power. But if their hearts be pure, they must all one day awaken to the fact that more than faith is required and more knowledge is at hand.

But, precious ones, many along life's way have come to the point where they knew there must be something more for them to have, to glean, and to know whereby they could fulfill their mission. And they have hunted and searched for someone to tell them the right course, and they have not found. For the Teachings were not available, they were not spread abroad in the land. And you yourselves in past embodiments have searched for Truth and have not found it. And sometimes, in despair, you have accepted substitutes that have led you down the pathway to more karma and the round of involvement in human affairs.

The Mercy of the Law Is Extended to You

In this service that you are rendering through this activity you find that there is taking place in your forcefield the atonement for all ignorance and past error that you performed as you knew not what you did. And by the grace of God and the mercy of his Law, there is extended unto you, therefore, the opportunity not only to atone for your own past ignorance, but to provide for mankind the way whereby they might also come to the knowledge of the Truth, by which they may also atone for their past errors.

And so, you see, the accomplishment of this mission for the Christ, of this service for humanity is very important to the world. And a great deal depends upon its fulfillment. For succeeding generations, if they are fired by illumination and the flame and desire to know Truth, may come to the fountain.

Let us pray that the fountain be not dry, that they will find the living waters of Truth because you have determined to leave behind footsteps upon the sands of life, waymarks of progress, and books, lessons, dictations in printed form that will teach mankind the Way.

Your Are a Link in the Chain of Being

Realize, then, that you are the missing link between the era of the Christ and the era of the golden age. And if you can weld together the mighty chain of the saints of all ages, which has temporarily been broken by man's inattention to liberty and to cosmic precepts, you will be forging the chain of Being that will unlock for generations for all time to come the mighty precepts of life that are the keys to their immortal victory.

The entire Spirit of the Great White Brotherhood pours forth gratitude to those who have thus served in the holy cause this day, even as our hearts are filled with gratitude from your octave from the sons and daughters of light who are receiving the powerful words in printed form that are released through this activity.

You are not always there to listen as the heart leaps, as the Holy Christ Self rejoices upon the contact of the outer self with the higher truths that are locked in his own Christ identity. And even the body elemental jumps up and down for glee as followers of the greater light of God come into a knowledge whereby they might integrate themselves and find wholeness and greater reunion with the mighty I AM Presence.

Your Mission Is Important

I wanted to tell you this day how important your mission is, then, to the bringing of Truth unto mankind. For the most part the evolutions of this planet live in a world that is seventy-five to eighty-five percent a lie, a mirage—almost like a movie set. And they do not know the Truth, especially behind the Iron Curtain where life is turned upside down and distorted for the people who are attempting there to serve what they think to be the highest principle.

Beloved ones, without Truth, without the key of this science, there is much that mankind will lose. That they do not lose the precious heritage that we have to pass on is our desire. It is our gift.

And we pledge ourselves this day anew to uphold this activity, to uphold all serving it and all members of it who are sincere, that by the holding forth of these outposts of light across the planet there may be established bulwarks of freedom and a place of refuge where the holy precepts of Truth might be held forth until mankind come of age.

That they come of age through various activities that we have sponsored is well and good, and your very decrees and prayers go forth as a flood tide of light to uplift mankind wherever they may be. In the lowest reaches of degradation unto the highest ivory towers of learning, mankind are taken a little bit higher, a little bit further upon the way of finding their own reunion with God as you join to pray each day.

I take my leave of you this hour, but there is much more that I would like to bring to you. I pray, therefore, that your consecration to Truth shall be of such magnitude that I may return and talk with you even as I had the privilege of teaching and preaching in my life as Paul. For the hours

of communion and of association with the followers of Christ, as heart to heart the knowledge
of the Law is imparted, these are sacred, these are
precious. These are locked in the eternal memory
of every ascended being. And so, I look forward
to coming again.

I bless you in his name and I fire within your
hearts a portion of our flame.

I thank you. ⚜

January 8, 1967
Colorado Springs, Colorado

Mantras for Healing

The following decrees and mantras can be used to invoke the light of healing. After giving the preamble, give your own personal prayer for healing, naming the specific condition or individual that requires healing. Remember to ask that healing might be accomplished according to the highest good of the soul and according to God's will.

Additional decrees may be found on the following pages of this book: "More Violet Fire," page 111; "Forgiveness," page 131; "The Law of Forgiveness," page 132; and "Living Truth," page 147.

For more information on the use of decrees and mantras, along with specific visualizations for healing, see Mark L. Prophet and Elizabeth Clare Prophet, *The Science of the Spoken Word.*

Violet Fire and Tube of Light Decree

O my constant, loving I AM Presence, thou light of God above me whose radiance forms a circle of fire before me to light my way:

I AM faithfully calling to thee to place a great pillar of light from my own mighty I AM God Presence all around me right now today! Keep it intact through every passing moment, manifesting as a shimmering shower of God's beautiful light through which nothing human can ever pass. Into this beautiful electric circle of divinely charged energy direct a swift upsurge of the violet fire of freedom's forgiving, transmuting flame!

Cause the ever expanding energy of this flame projected downward into the forcefield of my human energies to completely change every negative condition into the positive polarity of my own great God Self! Let the magic of its mercy so purify my world with light that all whom I contact shall always be blessed with the fragrance of violets from God's own heart in memory of the blessed dawning day when all discord—cause, effect, record and memory—is forever changed into the victory of light and the peace of the ascended Jesus Christ.

I AM now constantly accepting the full power and manifestation of this fiat of light and calling it into instantaneous action by my own God-given free will and the power to accelerate without limit this sacred release of assistance from God's own heart until all men are ascended and God-free in the light that never, never, never fails!

Traveling Protection

Lord Michael before,
Lord Michael behind,
Lord Michael to the right,
Lord Michael to the left,
Lord Michael above,
Lord Michael below,
Lord Michael, Lord Michael
    wherever I go!
I AM his love protecting here!
I AM his love protecting here!
I AM his love protecting here!

Lord Michael

In the name of the beloved mighty victorious Presence of God, I AM in me, my very own beloved Holy Christ Self, Holy Christ Selves of all mankind, beloved Archangel Michael, beloved Lanello, the entire Spirit of the Great White Brotherhood and the World Mother, elemental life—fire, air, water and earth! I decree:

1. Lord Michael, Lord Michael,
     I call unto thee—
   Wield thy sword of blue flame
     And now cut me free!

Refrain: Blaze God-power, protection
     Now into my world,
   Thy banner of faith
     Above me unfurl!
   Transcendent blue lightning
     Now flash through my soul,
   I AM by God's mercy
     Made radiant and whole!

2. Lord Michael, Lord Michael,
     I love thee, I do—
   With all thy great faith
     My being imbue!

3. Lord Michael, Lord Michael
   And legions of blue—
   Come seal me, now keep me
   Faithful and true!

Coda: I AM with thy blue flame
      Now full-charged and blest,
      I AM now in Michael's
      Blue-flame armor dressed!   (3x)

And in full faith I consciously accept this manifest, manifest, manifest! (3x) right here and now with full power, eternally sustained, all-powerfully active, ever expanding and world enfolding until all are wholly ascended in the light and free!

Beloved I AM! Beloved I AM! Beloved I AM!

Strip Us of All Doubt and Fear

Beloved mighty victorious Presence of God, I AM in me, O thou beloved immortal victorious threefold flame of eternal Truth within my heart, Holy Christ Selves of all mankind, beloved Saint Germain, beloved El Morya, beloved Jesus the Christ, beloved Mother Mary, beloved Archangel Michael, beloved Ray-O-Light, beloved mighty Astrea, beloved Lanello, the entire Spirit of the

Great White Brotherhood and the World Mother,
elemental life—fire, air, water and earth!

In the name of the Presence of God which
I AM and through the magnetic power of the
sacred fire vested in me, which I am consciously
qualifying with the fearlessness flame, I decree:

Strip us of all doubt and fear,   (3x)
   Beloved great I AM.
Strip us of all doubt and fear,   (3x)
   Flood us with oceans of fearlessness flame.
Strip us of all doubt and fear,   (3x)
   Remove each human cause and core.
Strip us of all doubt and fear,   (3x)
   Give us faith never known before.
Strip us of all doubt and fear,   (3x)
   Give violet-ray freedom to all today.
Strip us of all doubt and fear,   (3x)
   In Victory's light sustain our might.
Strip us of all doubt and fear,   (3x)
   By cosmic I AM fire, manifest thy desire.
Strip us of all doubt and fear,   (3x)
   Command the earth now free.
Strip us of all doubt and fear,   (3x)
   Ascend us all to thee.

And in full faith...

Decree to Beloved Mighty Astrea— "The Starry Mother"

In the name of the beloved mighty victorious Presence of God, I AM in me, mighty I AM Presence and Holy Christ Selves of all mankind, by and through the magnetic power of the sacred fire vested in the threefold flame burning within my heart, I call to beloved Mighty Astrea and Purity, beloved Lanello, the entire Spirit of the Great White Brotherhood and the World Mother, elemental life—fire, air, water and earth! to lock your cosmic circles and swords of blue flame in, through and around: my four lower bodies, my electronic belt, my heart chakra and all of my chakras, my entire consciousness, being and world. [name conditions or individuals that require healing]

Cut me loose and set me free (3x) from all that is less than God's perfection and my own divine plan fulfilled.

> 1. O beloved Astrea, may God Purity
>   Manifest here for all to see,
>   God's divine will shining through
>   Circle and sword of brightest blue.

1st chorus: Come now answer this my call,
Lock thy circle round us all.
Circle and sword of brightest blue,
Blaze now, raise now, shine right through!

2. Cutting life free from patterns unwise,
Burdens fall off while souls arise
Into thine arms of infinite love,
Merciful shining from heaven above.

3. Circle and sword of Astrea now shine,
Blazing blue-white my being refine,
Stripping away all doubt and fear,
Faith and goodwill patterns appear.

2nd chorus: Come now answer this my call,
Lock thy circle round us all.
Circle and sword of brightest blue,
Raise our youth now, blaze right through!

3rd chorus: Come now answer this my call,
Lock thy circle round us all.
Circle and sword of brightest blue,
Raise mankind now, shine right through!

And in full faith...

N.B. Give the decree once, using the first chorus after each verse.
Give it a second time, using the second chorus after each verse.
Give it a third time, using the third chorus after each verse. These
three sets of three verses followed by each of the three choruses
comprise one giving of the decree, or one Astrea pattern.

Flame of Healing

Beloved mighty victorious Presence of God, I AM in me, thou threefold flame of eternal Truth within my heart, Holy Christ Selves of all mankind, beloved Hilarion, Pallas Athena, Archangel Raphael and the healing angels, beloved Lanello, the entire Spirit of the Great White Brotherhood and the World Mother, elemental life—fire, air, water and earth!

In the name of the Presence of God which I AM and through the magnetic power of the sacred fire vested in me, I decree:

1. Healing flame of brightest green,
   I AM God Presence all serene,
   Through me pour thy mercy light,
   Now let Truth make all things right.

Refrain: Flame of consecration wonder,
   Let my mind on thee now ponder
   Service to my brother stronger
       And the fullness of thy power.
   Flame of consecration healing,
   Keep my being full of healing,
   Mercy to my brothers sealing
       By the grace of God desire.

2. Flame of healing, fill my form,
   Vibrant life in me reborn;
   God within me, make me whole,
   I AM healing every soul.

And in full faith...

Come We Now before Thy Flame

In the name of the beloved mighty victorious Presence of God which I AM and by and through the magnetic power of the sacred fire vested in the threefold flame burning within my heart, beloved Lanello, the entire Spirit of the Great White Brotherhood and the World Mother, elemental life—fire, air, water and earth! I decree:

O Cyclopea, Jesus dear,
   Mother Mary so sincere,
Come we now before thy flame
   To be healed in God's own name.
Stand we in this place in time
   Invoking now thy healing chime!

Tone of golden radiance
   Tinged with brilliant healing green,
Pouring comfort through the earth,
   Perfection so serene!

Come, O love in holy action,
Give us now God-satisfaction.
By the power of holy healing
In perfection's flame now sealing!

I AM holding _____ (give name or names) _____
    Before thy Presence here;
Shed thy love ray forth upon ____ (him, her, them) ,
    Release thy blessing dear!

    And in full faith...

_____

The flame of healing is a brilliant emerald green, and it should be visualized as a pulsating flame around the one for whom you are seeking God's healing. This healing flame of brilliant green is used in conjunction with the violet flame. The violet flame is for the removal of the cause and core of the condition, and the healing flame is for the bringing of God's energies within one's temple into alignment once again.

Notes

Books referenced here are published by Summit
University Press unless indicated otherwise.

NOTES TO SECTION I
  1. Acts 9:3–9.
  2. Acts 9:17.
  3. Acts 9:18.
  4. Hilarion, "A Door of Utterance," *Pearls of Wisdom*,
     vol. 23, no. 5, February 3, 1980.
  5. Gal. 1:11–17, Jerusalem Bible.
  6. Hilarion, October 7, 1990, "Preach the Gospel of
     Salvation in Every Nation!" *Pearls of Wisdom*, vol.
     33, no. 39, October 7, 1990.
  7. II Cor. 12:1, 7, 8–10.
  8. Acts 17:22–23, 29–33.
  9. Acts 18:9–10.
 10. Acts 18:8.
 11. Acts 21:27–28.
 12. Acts 28:4.
 13. Sanat Kumara, *The Opening of the Seventh Seal*
     (Gardiner, Mont.: The Summit Lighthouse Library,
     2001), pp. 271, 272.
 14. Acts 21:4, 11–14.

15. Jesus, April 3, 1983, "The Glorification of the Son of God," *Pearls of Wisdom,* vol. 26, no. 35, August 28, 1983.

16. Acts 9:5.

17. Hilarion, December 29, 1976, "The Personal Saviour, The Personal Guru," in Mark L. Prophet and Elizabeth Clare Prophet, *Lords of the Seven Rays* (1986), book 2, pp. 171–73.

18. II Cor. 12:4.

19. Col. 1:27.

20. Hilarion, December 29, 1977, "Transference of the Healing Flame," in Mark L. Prophet and Elizabeth Clare Prophet, *Lords of the Seven Rays* (1986), book 1, pp. 203–4.

21. In Paul's time, individuals were required to balance all of their karma before qualifying for the ascension. Since the inauguration of the New Dispensation early in the twentieth century, it has been possible to ascend having balanced at least 51 percent of one's karma, the remaining portion being balanced on inner levels after the ascension.

22. Hilarion, "The Revolution of Truth."

23. Herbert Thurston and Donald Atwater, eds., *Butler's Lives of the Saints,* rev. (New York: P. J. Kenedy and Sons, 1962), 4:163.

24. Matt. 10:8.

25. Hilarion, "The Personal Saviour, The Personal Guru," *Lords of the Seven Rays,* book 2, p. 181.

26. The ascension comes at the conclusion of lifetimes of the soul's service to life. The prerequisites for this graduation from earth's schoolroom are: (1) The soul must become one with her Christ Self; (2) She must balance at least 51 percent of her karma; and (3) She

must fulfill her mission on earth according to her divine plan.

27. II Kings 2: 13–14.
28. Hilarion, "The Personal Saviour, The Personal Guru," *Lords of the Seven Rays,* book 2, p. 175.
29. Hilarion, January 1, 1995, "A Campaign on Behalf of the Children of the World," *Pearls of Wisdom,* vol. 38, no. 7, February 12, 1995.
30. Matt. 24:14; Mark 13:10.
31. Hilarion, October 7, 1990, "Preach the Gospel of Salvation in Every Nation," *Pearls of Wisdom,* vol. 33, no. 39, October 7, 1990.
32. Hilarion, "The Personal Saviour, The Personal Guru," *Lords of the Seven Rays,* book 2, p. 185.
33. Hilarion, "Classes and Initiation in Truth at the Temple in Crete," in Elizabeth Clare Prophet, *The Opening of the Temple Doors* (2003), pp. 63–65.
34. John 8:32.
35. Hilarion, July 9, 1967.

NOTES TO SECTION II

1. Phil. 4:8.
2. Hilarion, January 8, 1967, "The Gift of Divine Healing," published in Section III of this book.
3. Ibid.
4. Hilarion, October 10, 1966.
5. Hilarion, January 1, 1995, "A Campaign on Behalf of the Children of the World," *Pearls of Wisdom,* vol. 38, no. 7, February 12, 1995.
6. John 9:1–7.
7. John 5:4.
8. Hilarion, December 30, 1974, in Mark L. Prophet and Elizabeth Clare Prophet, *Lords of the Seven Rays*

(1986), book 1, pp. 210–11.

9. Ibid., pp. 211–12.

10. Ibid., p. 213.

11. Hilarion, "Understanding the Kingdom of Self," *Pearls of Wisdom,* vol. 15, no. 9, February 27, 1972.

12. Hilarion, July 9, 1967, in Mark L. Prophet and Elizabeth Clare Prophet, *Lords of the Seven Rays* (1986), book 1, pp. 214–16.

13. Hilarion, December 30, 1974.

14. After his ascension in 1684, Saint Germain received a special dispensation from the Lords of Karma to return to earth in a physical body. He was known to the courts of Europe in the eighteenth and nineteenth centuries as le Comte de Saint Germain. He was called the "Wonderman of Europe" for his miraculous abilities, which included bilocation, appearing at court and then dissolving his form at will, removing flaws from diamonds and other precious stones, and precipitating an elixir that prevented aging. For further information about the Wonderman of Europe, see *Saint Germain—Master Alchemist,* another volume in the *Meet the Master* series.

15. Saint Germain, April 16, 1988, quoted in Elizabeth Clare Prophet, *The Astrology of the Four Horsemen: How You Can Heal Yourself and Planet Earth* (1991), pp. 528–29.

16. Saint Germain, "The Violet Transmuting Flame," in Mark L. Prophet and Elizabeth Clare Prophet, *The Science of the Spoken Word* (1991), pp. 107, 106.

17. El Morya, *The Chela and the Path* (1984), p. 63.

18. Hilarion, "The Gift of Divine Healing."

19. Matt. 9:5; Mark 2:9; Luke 5:23.

20. Luke 22:42.

21. Kuan Yin, October 10, 1969, "The Sword of Mercy," in *Crystallization of the God Flame*, vol. 2, no. 6.

22. Kuan Yin, January 21, 1968, "Karma, Mercy, and the Law," in *Kuan Yin Opens the Door to the Golden Age, Pearls of Wisdom 1982*, Book Two, p. 106.

23. Kuan Yin, April 10, 1974, "Mercy: The Fire That Tries Every Man's Works," in *Kuan Yin Opens the Door to the Golden Age, Pearls of Wisdom 1982*, Book Two, p. 95.

24. Matt. 10:16.

25. Kuan Yin, September 18, 1976, "A People and a Teaching Whose Time Has Come," in *Crystallization of the God Flame*, vol. 2, no. 7.

26. Kuan Yin, "Mercy: The Fire That Tries Every Man's Works," *Pearls of Wisdom 1982*, Book Two, p. 96.

27. Kuan Yin, December 15, 1974, "A Mother's-Eye View of the World," in *Kuan Yin Opens the Door to the Golden Age, Pearls of Wisdom 1982*, Book Two, p. 87.

28. Matt. 18:22.

29. Kuan Yin, "A Mother's-Eye View of the World," *Pearls of Wisdom 1982*, Book Two, p. 84.

30. Ibid.

31. Serapis Bey, *Dossier on the Ascension* (1978), p. 90.

32. Hilarion, "The Gift of Divine Healing."

33. Hilarion, January 1, 1995, "A Campaign on Behalf of the Children of the World," *Pearls of Wisdom*, vol. 38, no. 7, February 12, 1995.

34. Matt. 13:54–58; Mark 6:1–6.

35. John 8:32.

36. Hilarion, "Accumulation of Age-Old Errors Challenged," *Pearls of Wisdom*, vol. 11, no. 5, February 4,

1968.

37. Hilarion, December 30, 1974.

38. Hilarion, August 29, 1982, "The Power of Conversion," in *Pearls of Wisdom,* vol. 25, no. 63, 1982.

39. Matt. 6:10.

40. Matt. 24:28; Hilarion, "The Personal Saviour, The Personal Guru," *Lords of the Seven Rays,* book 2, p. 184.

**Other Books by Mark L. Prophet
and Elizabeth Clare Prophet**

The Masters and Their Retreats

Lords of the Seven Rays

Fallen Angels and the Origins of Evil

*Saint Germain's Prophecy for the
New Millennium*

Saint Germain On Alchemy

Keys to the Kingdom

Violet Flame to Heal Body, Mind & Soul

Karma and Reincarnation

The Story of Your Soul

The Path of Brotherhood

The Chela and the Path

The Human Aura

The Opening of the Temple Doors

Alchemy of the Heart

Access the Power of Your Higher Self

Creative Abundance

Your Seven Energy Centers

How to Work with Angels

The Creative Power of Sound

For More Information

Summit University Press books are available at
fine bookstores everywhere. A wide selection
of our titles has been translated into a total
of 31 languages.
We invite you to download a free catalog of
Summit University Press books, eBooks, CDs
and DVDs at

www.SummitUniversityPress.com

or contact us at

Summit University Press/
The Summit Lighthouse Library
63 Summit Way, Gardiner, MT 59030 USA

1-800-245-5445 or 1-406-848-9500
Fax: 1-800-221-8307 or 1-406-848-9555

www.SummitUniversityPress.com
www.YouTube.com/SummitUnivPress
www.facebook.com/SummitUniversityPress

E-mail: info@SummitUniversityPress.com

Mark L. Prophet and Elizabeth Clare Prophet are world-renowned authors. Among their best-sellers are *The Lost Years of Jesus: Documentary Evidence of Jesus' 17-Year Journey to the East,* the four-book series of *The Lost Teachings of Jesus, Saint Germain On Alchemy* and the landmark series Climb the Highest Mountain.®

They have pioneered techniques of modern spirituality, including the use of the creative power of sound for personal growth and world transformation. A wide selection of their books is translated into a total of thirty-one languages.

The unpublished works of Mark L. Prophet and Elizabeth Clare Prophet continue to be published by Summit University Press.